Wanderlush

To Loraine—

Thanks so much for the support. I hope you enjoy.

David Pehot

Wanderlush

DAVID ROBERT

abbott press

Abbott Press books may be ordered through booksellers or by contacting:

Abbott Press
1663 Liberty Drive
Bloomington, IN 47403
www.abbottpress.com
Phone: 1-866-697-5310

ISBN: 978-1-4582-1741-7 (sc)
ISBN: 978-1-4582-1740-0 (hc)
ISBN: 978-1-4582-1739-4 (e)

Library of Congress Control Number: 2014948572

Printed in the United States of America.

Abbott Press rev. date: 08/08/2014

This book is dedicated to my sisters, Kelly and Lisa, my partner, Pete, and my mom, who graciously allowed me to have fun at their expense.

CONTENTS

France (2006)

United Arab Emirates (2010)

CHAPTER 1

Newton's Law of Motion

"David?"

The shrill of the nurse's voice woke me from a daydream. I had worn myself out after an hour of nervously waiting to see my gastroenterologist, whom I fully expected would confirm my suspicion that I'd be dead from ass cancer before the end of the month. I had no legitimate reason to suspect I was dying of cancer, other than the fact that I suffered from severe hypochondria and I had previously failed on separate occasions to convince my family and friends that I was dying of lupus, mad cow disease, Radon poisoning, and Ebola. Besides, my health insurance covered colonoscopies in full after age thirty, so what did I have to lose? Thirty seconds after walking into my doctor's office, I received my diagnosis: irritable bowel syndrome. I am convinced irritable bowel syndrome is the catch-all diagnosis that gastroenterologists dish out to patients who confess to having a nutty mother.

"Damn it!" I shouted.

"I thought you'd be relieved," my doctor said.

I *was* relieved to learn I wasn't dying, even though I knew the odds of it happening were infinitesimally small. I just wish I had known before I called my mother and offered to take her on a series of "good-bye" vacations before my being sent off to hospice, where a small group of dedicated volunteers would keep vigil at my bedside and read excerpts from *Chicken Soup for the Terminally Ill*. It's shocking what you'll do and say when you think you're dying of ass cancer. After my mother reassured me that it was more plausible I would die at the hands of Pete, my partner of ten years, once he's finally had enough of my histrionics, she accepted my invitation. *What the hell was I thinking?*

I describe my mother as a cross between Bea Arthur and Karen Walker from *Will and Grace*. She is notorious for bending the rules but more so for nursing a hefty glass of chardonnay all day. If my mother were a product, her tagline would be *Proudly raising hell since 1945*. She's also the person my family turns to for honest feedback. Coincidentally, the feedback becomes more honest as the wine in her glass diminishes.

I often wondered how the universe brought the two of us together. The answer, surprisingly, is Newton's Law of Motion. Anyone who has taken a basic physics class is familiar with the theory, which in part explains that for every action there is an equal but opposite reaction. I tend to think of the theory as the science behind why people like me are born to mothers like mine. On the morning of June 21, 1970, when my mother sauntered into the local hospital, hurled her pregnant body onto the first available gurney, lit a Virginia Slims 100, and yelled, "Let's get this over with. I have a pinochle tournament tonight" (the action), she sealed her fate by giving the universe permission to deliver someone like me into the world (the reaction).

Several years passed before my mother got a taste of the "equal reaction" part of the theory. Some children are fortunate enough to inherit large sums of money from their mother, while others acquire an uncanny ability to spell words like *phenobarbital* before age six or master the clarinet before they are fully potty trained. I got anxiety and obsessive-compulsive disorder. While my childhood friends played whiffle ball and tag in the field down the street from my house, I hid under my bed, waiting for the Cold War to end. No wonder I was the target of bullies from shortly after birth through my late thirties.

Don't get me wrong; my mother is the absolute sweetest woman you will ever meet. She'd give someone the shirt off her back, and she often has done so at dinner parties and other functions where this would be considered, at the very least, inappropriate. That's why I love her. And she is fiercely protective. On the rare occasions when I allowed the bullying to affect me, my mother would attempt to comfort me by saying, "Remember, dear, you are the sperm that beat the others in the race. So the next time those kids bully you, turn around and run like hell."

I give my mother a lot of credit for having four children. The concept of raising a child was foreign to Pete and me. We weren't opposed to the idea of having a child; we simply couldn't find anyone with an adequate answer to our question, "Who the hell is going to feed and clothe it for the first eighteen years?" We liked the idea of having children; we just didn't want any of the responsibility and drama. Pete and I continue to leave open the opportunity that the proverbial stork might swoop in late on a Thursday night after *American Idol* and drop off at our doorstep a healthy, self-sufficient, and neutered eighteen-year-old who planned to leave for university, on a full scholarship, the following Tuesday.

I'll admit that although I was the third child, it took some time for my mom to warm up to me. I don't think she was fully prepared for a child who could go toe to toe with her so early. At age ten I learned an important lesson regarding the depth of my mother's humor and just how far she was willing to go to pay me back for the continuous stress I placed her under.

One weekend day I caught a few minutes of the Jerry Lewis telethon, which was a wildly popular annual televised fundraiser that comedian Jerry Lewis hosted. In that telethon Jerry interviewed children who were battling illness, showed clips of their story, and periodically appealed to the viewing audience to give to "Jerry's kids." This signature phrase became part of America's lexicon. So given that my own father's name was Jerry, I devised a plan to canvas my neighborhood collecting money for none other than Jerry's kids. I just neglected to tell my neighbors that it wasn't Jerry Lewis's kids I was collecting money for but rather my father's kids, and more precisely me.

Well, I thought I had hit the jackpot until my mother found a large stash of candy in my bedroom and questioned how I had gotten it. I had no choice but to confess. My mother was not pleased, and she felt I owed each neighbor a face-to-face apology. I was embarrassed, to say the least, to be forced to retrace my steps to return the money I had collected. My mother walked me to each house and made me knock on the front door and apologize. The first visit didn't go so well, because my apology fell well short of my mother's expectations.

"I'm sorry, Mrs. Johnson. Even though I still feel strongly that I technically didn't lie, the collection tin should have clearly been labeled with Jerry *Robert's* kids. I apologize for the confusion, and to set things right I'm returning your donation."

My mother leaned on my shoulder and pushed me against Mrs. Johnson. I was immediately overpowered by the scent of patchouli and secondhand smoke. "Is that all, David?" I should have shut my mouth then, but I couldn't help myself. Before my mother could whip me off Mrs. Johnson's front steps, I was off and running.

"Oh, yes, thank you, Mother," I added as I looked up at Mrs. Johnson. "I'd like to take this opportunity to ask if you would be interested in rolling your donation into a fund to help the homeless. This is a fund that is dear to my heart as I have a strong suspicion I'll be homeless by the end of the day."

Anger radiated from my mother's face, but to her credit I thought she closed the conversation with a brilliant display of control. She stepped in front of me and added, "It's becoming clearer to us that a serious mistake was made at the hospital, and with your permission I'd like to use your donation to help set up a fund to get my real son back." She used that line at nearly every house, and we walked away with over seventy percent of the original donations. I wasn't sure if I should be offended or impressed, but either way I felt it was time well spent together. Little did I know that my mother planned to use that fund to send me to Saturday Catholic school. My mother always gets even.

Side note: I don't know what my mother was thinking by putting me in Catholic school, especially when she had shared with my father on more than one occasion that if I was ever to step into a confession booth it would likely require an intervention from the Vatican. In my opinion, she was asking for trouble.

Not long after my walk of shame through the neighborhood, each student in my Catholic school class (yes, she actually followed through on her threat) was asked to design a product that would make Jesus more relevant to young people. Having recently come off the Jerry Lewis stunt, I felt my innovative juices rising to an all-time high. I nearly jumped out of my khakis on the way home from class. I saw this assignment as a clear opportunity to shine.

I quickly designed a few product prototypes, most notably bubblegum-flavored communion wafers and Father May I, the board game. Even I thought the latter was a bit tasteless, so I eventually landed on Rice Christies. The tagline was *Put a little snap, crackle, and Pope into your morning*. I thought the product was genius and that it had a solid chance to eventually go to market. For the week leading up to my presentation I had vivid daydreams of every child in America waking up to a big bowl of Jesus.

Unfortunately, the nun who taught the class didn't share my enthusiasm. I didn't know this at the time, but apparently Catholic school is not the ideal place for children with an overactive imagination. I don't recall exactly what the nun, who my friends and I referred to as The Sister of Darkness, told my mother, but it was something along the lines of, "I would strongly suggest your son divert some of his sinful energy into prayer, because he's going to need it." Again, I should have kept my mouth shut, but I had to add my two cents.

"This was my mother's idea," I cried as my teacher looked at me with disapproving eyes.

My mother's jaw dropped. "David? Don't lie near a church!" She used the word *near* because technically we weren't in a church but rather in a classroom on the opposite side of the church parking lot. That's likely the reason why I didn't burst into flames when I dropped the F-bomb after my fellow students laughed at my product idea. The person responsible for designing the church property knew what he was doing.

I wiped the manufactured tears from my cheeks and purposely made my chin quiver as I looked up at my teacher. "I'm ten years old," I said. "Do you think someone my age could design a product so disrespectful to the church and to our savior?"

The nun gave my mother the look of death. My mother waited a moment, stared at me intensely as if to suggest *You really shouldn't have gone there*, and then began to plot her revenge. "I think it would be in everyone's best interest if you directed me to the person here who is responsible for exorcisms," my mother said as she placed herself between my teacher and me.

The nun took my mother's hands and smiled gently. "Right this way, Mrs. Robert."

The exorcism never happened, but I have to admit I spent the better part of that year on my best behavior, because I truly believed at any moment someone would knock at my door, and I'd be greeted by a gangly, elderly man with cold hands who would carry me away in a creepy hearse with lace curtains in the back windows. And I knew all too well that my mother always gets even.

Eventually, I didn't need to be near my mother to cause trouble. My driver's license test is a perfect example. I had just turned sixteen when I completed my driver's education course and was eligible for the driving test. In the car with me for the assessment were an overweight state police officer and my driver's education coach, Mr. Winters. Mr. Winters was a frail, anxious man, and the fact that he had survived forty hours with me during the training course was a shock to everyone, including him. On the ride to the test site, he had a few words of advice for me.

"Do what you are asked, don't say anything unless prompted, and please don't screw this up. I've never had a student fail the driver's test." I don't know if he got a bonus for each student who passed, but it seemed like a desperate plea to me.

The test went quite well until the last ten minutes. The police officer had me stop on a steep hill and asked me to perform a three-point turn. *Is this guy out of his mind?* I thought. I stopped the car for a moment to contemplate his request and then sped up the hill. "Why the hell would I do a three-point turn on this hill when I can pull into someone's driveway to turn around?" I said. And that is exactly what I did. I felt Mr. Winters sink into his seat.

When I pulled into the parking lot adjacent to the police station, the officer pointed to a parking space on the side of the lot and asked me to parallel park the car. I noticed a spot up ahead that didn't require parallel parking, so I quickly diverted the car into that space. As I pulled into it, I looked at the police officer and said, "I don't really like to parallel park, and so I'm content to continue driving around the lot looking for a space like this one." I poked the officer's bulging belly. "And look, I got you a couple of feet closer to the front door!" Mr. Winters sighed. The officer took out his pen, made a few notes on his notepad, and then had these words for me:

"I've been conducting driver's tests for twenty years, and I have to say I've never met someone quite like you before."

"I get that a lot," I replied.

The officer pulled his sunglasses down and stared at me. "You didn't complete any of the required elements, and you're language was colorful, to say the least. But you're innovative, and good drivers are able to think quickly. I'm passing you. Good luck." And with that, the officer opened the passenger door and stepped out.

"You're giving him a license?" cried Mr. Winters. "God help us."

I was thrilled. I made eye contact with Mr. Winters in the rearview mirror. "At least your record isn't blemished."

And so it went. I sped my way out of adolescence and into early adulthood. In case you are curious, I didn't parallel park a car until I was thirty-one, and even then it was under great pressure and duress. My mother directed me from the sidewalk. This, by the way, is the same woman who nearly failed her own driver's test for "palming" the wheel with one hand while holding a lit cigarette in the other during the parallel parking requirement.

When I wasn't torturing my mother or giving her reasons to disown me, I dreamed of traveling. I have an insatiable fascination with geography and maps. It was no surprise, though, that my desire to travel was stymied by the very quality that bonded my mother and me—anxiety. My mom and I will forever be connected by an irrational fear of flying. Well, okay, the fear is not related to flying as much as it is to crashing. The thought of hitting the ground at five hundred miles per hour and having my torso end up on someone's front porch and my toes scattered across someone else's backyard three states away is rather unsettling. Maybe that's just me.

A more plausible source of my wanderlust is the fear of missing out on something. To me, the risk of missing out on an experience far outweighs the risks associated with exploration. The risk was a selfish motivator, but it was good enough to persuade me to repeatedly get on an airplane with the ball of nerves I affectionately refer to as my mom.

Portugal (2002)

CHAPTER 2

Hard Candy

"O h, my God," I said as we boarded the plane in Boston. "I see two bolts missing from the door."

"Who cares, you freak," replied my sister, Lisa, as she pushed her way past me. "There's like a hundred more on there."

I was disappointed by my sister's response, and quite frankly I began to regret inviting her along with my mom and me. She and I were close in age. I was twenty months older, but we were polar opposites when it came to our personality. She is a pragmatic, no-bullshit kind of person. I am driven by emotion and found pleasure in overreacting. I liken Lisa to a honey badger. She's afraid of nothing and, although she looks sweet and innocent, she wouldn't hesitate to chew both of your legs off if you rubbed her the wrong way.

I preferred traveling with people like my mom, people who chewed Xanax like Tic Tacs and relentlessly sweated the small stuff. I wasn't even remotely ready at that early point in the vacation to hear a voice of reason.

Pete was our original choice of travel companion, but shortly after I booked the trip, he received deployment orders from his military unit, so I swapped him out for the only other person I knew who was crazy enough to travel with my mom and me. Pete was being sent overseas for at least several months, and the exact whereabouts of his eventual destination were to remain classified. I should have felt depressed or sad that I'd be away from Pete for so long, but instead I was pissed that he wouldn't tell me the location of his deployment. The secrecy within the military is precisely the reason I never tried out for a position. I hated being kept out of a secret.

Side note: For future reference, if I'm ever entrusted with classified information that, if revealed, could jeopardize national security, we're all screwed.

To Pete's credit, he kept that secret for the entire month leading up to his departure despite daily inquiries from me, my mom, and two of Pete's closest friends (I had to try every angle!). He's so trustworthy, which I think is one of his biggest flaws. When Pete dropped the three of us off at the airport, I leaned into him and said, "Call me when you settle in to wherever it is that you are going."

Pete snapped back, "David, I'm going to war, not the Four Seasons."

∞

"Besides, I'd be more worried if the plane was missing a wing," Lisa said as she shouldered her way down the aisle toward our seats. There was that damn voice of reason again. I didn't want Lisa to see me fighting off an emerging panic attack, but I leaned down anyway to look out the windows on both sides of the airplane. I was relieved to see two wings.

"Should I place my carry-on in the overhead compartment or under my seat?" my mom asked us as we settled into our seats. We were flying in a Boeing 757, which had three seats on each side of the aisle. My sister claimed the window seat, and my mom claimed the aisle, leaving me to squeeze into the center.

"Where are your Xanax?" I asked in return.

She dropped her bag onto her seat. "In my carry-on."

I glanced at the bag. I wasn't exactly sure how my mom was going to shove that bag under her seat. The carry-on was an overstuffed lime green quilted purse that had to weigh fifty pounds. But I wanted to keep those pills close by. "Keep the bag under your seat," I said. "I have a strong feeling we're going to need those pills sooner than later."

My mother's lack of organization is trumped only by her short-term memory loss. She can't remember shit. After we settled in, my mother began to paw through her carry-on for the Xanax I begged her to bring. "Damn! I can't remember where I put those pills," she said. Normally, I would bring my own pills, but I realized after we left the house earlier that day I had forgotten to refill my prescription. I'm hoping short-term memory loss isn't hereditary.

My mom could sense my panic. "What's the rush?" she asked.

She obviously hadn't looked at me since we sat down. I was sweating and trying to fight back pre-flight jitters. I imagined that I looked like a heroin addict on day two at a methadone clinic. I had to sit on my hands to keep them from trembling. "Look at me. I'm one panic attack away from being placed on the heart transplant list."

My mom continued to dig through her bag. "If it makes you feel any better, I think there's a greater likelihood you'll end up on the liver transplant list first."

I felt the cargo door close beneath us. My mom jumped slightly and grasped her armrests. "Was that turbulence?" Her eyes were shut, and I could tell she was clenching her teeth.

"We haven't even left yet," Lisa said.

My mother didn't look convinced. She continued to tear through her bag and began to take items out and place them on my lap. "Here are my vitamin supplements," she said as she handed me a large plastic bottle. She took several more prescription bottles out of her purse and handed them to me. "And I think these are my cholesterol pills."

"Some of these are outdated," I said. My mother didn't flinch. "Are these even legal?"

"Don't be silly," she replied. "I'm a nurse." Every time I heard my mother say that I imagined some unfortunate patient in her examination room sweating profusely as she lunged toward him while wearing a white nursing bonnet and holding a urine cup and a hypodermic needle.

Technically, my mom didn't answer the question, but I left her alone as she continued to empty the bag. I had read somewhere that nurses have a forty percent higher rate of prescription drug abuse than the general population, but I knew that moment probably wasn't the right time to flex my trivia skills, especially when I was waiting patiently for a pill of my own. My sister, who had nodded off as we taxied toward the runway, was apparently awoken by the scent of stale prescription pills and fear.

"The two of you are like a scene from *Valley of the Dolls*," she said. "For Christ's sake, take your pills or get drunk, and let me get some rest." In addition to behaving like a honey badger, Lisa was a teetotaler, which if I understand correctly is someone who deals with stress the old-fashioned way, by actually dealing with it.

My mom pulled a bag of hard candies from her carry-on. "Oh, look!" she said as she held up the bag. "I didn't know I had candy in here." She leaned over me and smiled at my sister in surprise. My sister had a soft spot for candy. I never really got into it as an adult. I probably still harbored some guilt for having bought candy with the money I ripped off from my neighbors with my Jerry Lewis Ponzi scheme. And besides, why would I fill my daily caloric need with candy when I could leave room for wine?

As far back as I can remember, Lisa had a hard candy swishing around in her mouth. When I was growing up, my mother was sure Lisa would end up choking on a candy, so she would facilitate monthly Heimlich maneuver workshops for my other siblings and me. While my older siblings and I took turns feeling each other up, trying to locate the diaphragm, Lisa sat quietly on the couch rolling a hard candy across her front teeth with her tongue. And she never got a cavity. I, on the other hand, would take one sip of Kool-Aid, and the next day two of my teeth would fall out.

I've had to use the Heimlich maneuver only once in my life, and surprisingly it wasn't on Lisa. I had to use it a few years ago on our Jack Russell terrier, Sophie. Pete and I took Sophie to our friend Jasmine's apartment for a visit, and while we were there, Sophie quietly dragged a black dildo from Jasmine's bedroom into the living room, where she proceeded to bite off and choke on one of the dildo's rubber testicles. Jasmine (not her real name, as I want to remain friends with her, and Jasmine just seemed like the name of someone who would own a black dildo) was more upset about the lost testicle than she was about Sophie nearly asphyxiating on her white shag carpet.

Side note: I don't mean to seem insensitive, but let's face it. If you're fixing to use a thirteen-inch black dildo, do you really need both testicles?

"Please tell me you have the Xanax," I said to my mom.

"I know they're in here somewhere. Wait, here they are. Phew!" She opened the plastic prescription bottle and peered inside. "Uh-oh. There's only one left."

17

A seven-hour flight with only one Xanax was as serious as a missing wing. "Well, hand it over," I demanded.

"You'd take your mother's last pill from her?" she asked me.

I leaned into her so I could whisper directly into her right ear. "Let's put this into perspective. It's not like stealing shoes from a homeless person." I didn't mention this to my mom, but I would have gladly put her into a headlock and squeezed her into submission if it meant I didn't have to spend the next seven hours gasping at every patch of turbulence the plane encountered.

Side note: How could a woman who was terrified of flying bring only one Xanax? Did she think we were returning home on kayaks?

My mother held up her right hand and pretended to stroke the strings of a tiny violin. "Oh, you poor thing. I'll tell you what, I'll split it with you."

"Deal."

She snapped the pill into two pieces, surprisingly without much effort, and handed me my portion. "And next time, bring your own pills," she said. "You're a grown man."

In my opinion, it's that type of advice that has kept my mom from winning mother of the year. I swallowed my half without any water, and before I knew it we were in the air. Once we were able to move about the cabin, I got up to use the restroom. Fortunately, I was traveling with the self-proclaimed expert on the topic. My mom may have been robbed of mother of the year, but there was no denying her expertise in airplane lavatories.

"Hey, Mom, I'm getting up for a minute," I told her.

"You going to use the restroom?" Her excitement was significantly disproportionate to the occasion.

I hesitated for a moment. "Yes."

For as nervous as she was with air travel, a hearty conversation about airplane bathrooms was a source of comfort for her. I prepared myself for a lengthy exchange. She tugged on my shirt. "Well, let's huddle for a minute. I can give you some advice." My mother had just swallowed half a Xanax. Why she felt she was in a position to give sound advice was beyond me.

"I'm thirty-two. Do I really need advice on how to use the bathroom?"

My mom dropped the bag of hard candies she'd been nervously playing with and pulled me closer. "No, it's not advice on how to use the bathroom. It's advice on how to get into it."

I had no idea what she was talking about. My mother spent the next several minutes sharing data she had tucked away in her head about the airlines' initiative to reduce the size of airplane lavatories to make room for more revenue-generating seats. She was convinced this initiative was putting passengers at risk of injury as they tried to squeeze themselves into the tiny rooms.

"Don't become a statistic," she told me.

The effects of my half of Xanax had not kicked in yet, but based on the nuttiness coming from my mother's lips, I figured I was in for a hell of a ride. "I weigh a hundred and fifty pounds. I could qualify as a carry-on," I informed her. "I think I'll be okay."

My mom stood up so I could squeeze past her. "I think you're making a big mistake."

I initially waved off her appeal. I wasn't interested in how the bathrooms worked or how they were designed or how many people were injured each year trying to get in or out of them. I just wanted to pee. But my bladder was a lot smaller than her capacity to wear me down, so I gave in.

"Okay, what advice do you have?"

"The first thing you need to do is stretch," she told me. My mom lifted her right leg and placed her foot on her seat. Her left leg remained in the aisle while her torso faced the front of the plane. She looked like a sumo wrestler preparing to facilitate a birthing class. "Okay, here we go," she said as she listed significantly to the left. It wasn't your run-of-the-mill stretch; it was one of those stretches that you're certain will result in a wardrobe malfunction. My mother's dangling head caught the attention of the elderly man sitting in the seat across from her. They were so close to each other I'm fairly sure he caught a good whiff of her Xanax breath. "Hi there," she said with a tone that suggested she was in her own little world. "Just a little stretching going on here. Nothing to be alarmed about."

"Mom, are you ever going to retire that hideous lavender sweat suit?" My mom's go-to outfit for travel was a lavender sweat suit and white sneakers. She's worn the same outfit on road trips for as long as I can remember.

"They're comfortable. And besides, I wouldn't be able to do this deep a stretch if I was wearing something else."

To be honest, I wasn't sure she should be doing that stretch at all. She ignored the hints I threw at her using my body language and instead continued to bend and dip. I shifted back and forth uncomfortably.

"Are we through?" I asked.

My mother gently grabbed my arm. "Wait! Make sure when you enter the doorway you arch your back like a pole-vaulter."

"A pole-vaulter?" Clearly her half pill had kicked in.

"Yes! You know that arch they make when they clear the bar? That's the movement you want. Trust me on this one."

"I'll keep that in mind."

My mother gave me a thumbs-up for encouragement as I sprinted toward the bathroom. A few minutes later I returned to my seat. My mother noticed I was rubbing my lower back. "You didn't arch, did ya?"

I stared at her as if to suggest *Don't go there*. My mother was right. I should have arched my damn back, but there was no way in hell I was going to tell her. She would have talked about it for the remainder of the flight. My sister took advantage of the fact that my mom and I were out of our seat to get up to use the bathroom as well.

"Any advice for me, Mom?"

My mother was delighted at my sister's interest, so she spent the next few minutes providing a quick tutorial on the proper positioning of hands and feet to ensure a smooth entry into the lavatory. If I hadn't known the topic of discussion, I would have thought my mom was training my sister to be a mime. "When you close the door behind you, all you have to do is pivot your body, take your foot out of the sink, and drop into position. It works like a charm."

"That sounds dangerous."

My mom dismissed the remark. "Look what happened to your brother."

Lisa rolled her eyes and headed for the lavatory. She returned about five minutes later.

"How did it go?" asked my mom.

"I took your stupid advice. My left foot ended up in the toilet, and my ass ended up in the sink."

"Oooh. That's unfortunate," my mom said. "Maybe this plane's bathrooms haven't been reconfigured yet."

"Take another pill and go to sleep," Lisa said as she crawled into the row of seats.

Obviously, my sister hadn't overheard my mom and me fighting over the only pill she brought. As she passed over my mother's lap, my mom had to get in the last word.

"Your tush is still wet, sweetheart."

Lisa sighed heavily. "You're lucky I don't have gas."

CHAPTER 3

Pair of Teeth by the Dashboard Lights

Thankfully, the remainder of the flight was uneventful, and we landed safely in Lisbon. Before we left the U.S., I reserved a car through an online rental company. I had been looking for a cheap alternative to the mainstream rental agencies and landed on a company called Last Resort Car Rentals. Although the name was rather ominous, I decided to take the risk. I had no idea if someone would actually be waiting for us when we arrived. But sure enough, as we approached the car rental kiosk we noticed a plump, well-dressed, middle-aged man holding a sign with what appeared to be my name on it. The sign read "Dabid Rogert." The spelling was close enough for us, and besides I've been called much worse. We introduced ourselves, signed the required paperwork, and followed the man to the parking garage.

The agent was adamant about providing a brief driving lesson to prepare us for the congested roads in Lisbon. I tried to talk him out of it because we were tired and anxious to get to our hotel. But he was a persistent salesman, and after some moderate pushback, we gave in. I jumped into the passenger seat while my mother and sister piled into the back. Before we had a chance to secure our seatbelt, the seemingly easygoing rental agent stomped the gas pedal and tore out of the parking space like the space shuttle *Endeavor* leaving its launch pad.

The car sped through the garage toward the exit. "Jesus H. Christ!" my mother screamed.

Smoke billowed from the wheel wells as the car careened around a sharp corner. The agent swerved several times to avoid guardrails, lampposts, and shocked pedestrians. As we entered what I hoped was our final turn, the agent let go of the steering wheel and began the verbal portion of the lesson. I would have preferred he waited for all four tires to touch down before showing us the more commonly used international hand signals.

> *Side note: I don't think any of us gave a rat's ass at that point about how to notify other drivers that we might be backing up or exiting a roundabout. Besides, there's no hand signal in the world that grabs attention faster than a grandmother in the backseat swearing like a truck driver.*

"Dis is de vay," the driver shouted.

I barely heard him over the screeching of the tires. From what I could hear, his accent sounded more German than Portuguese, but I was in no position to question his ancestry.

"The way to where?" I asked, not really expecting an answer.

"Hopefully the emergency room," my mom shouted from the backseat.

I would have turned around to give my mom a reassuring glance, but the G force generated by our turn pinned my head against the seat. The driver took back control of the steering wheel and aimed the car toward the exit gate.

Is this really happening? I thought. "Do you think we could test the brakes?" I asked the driver as we approached the gate.

Surprisingly, the driver heard my plea and stomped on the brake pedal, causing the wheels to lock up. The car fishtailed.

"We're going to die!" cried Lisa. "And I haven't done any shopping here yet."

The car fishtailed a few more times and then came to an abrupt halt directly in front of the exit. Because of the sudden stop, bodies in motion stayed in motion, and my mother and sister found themselves jammed into the space between the two front seats. My chin rested on the cup holder that jutted from the dashboard, and my left leg was draped across the agent's lap. I lifted my head and noticed black smoke rushing from under the hood, and I could hear the faint sound of a hubcap rolling away from the car.

My mom freed herself and wiped her forehead with her sleeve. "Could you open the trunk, please?" she asked the agent as she blinked her eyes and shook her head to reorient herself. "I think part of my pelvis is back there."

My sister picked up an item from the floor of the car and handed it to my mom. "I think these might be your bottom teeth."

My mom jammed her teeth into her purse. "Is it legal to drink if the car isn't moving?" she asked the agent. He didn't respond. "I'll take that as a yes." She pulled a small bottle of chardonnay from her purse, twisted the cap off, and downed it in one swallow. "I'm almost too old for this shit."

I removed my leg from the agent's lap and turned to face my mom. "I'm not sure what's more disturbing, having your bottom teeth bounce off my lap or the fact that you had a bottle of chardonnay in your purse."

My mother reached into her purse and pulled out a single-serving bottle of red wine that she must have received from the flight attendant and handed it to me. "Still horrified?"

I snatched the bottle away from her and shoved it into my backpack. We spent the next few minutes reassembling my mother and the car. After both were in somewhat functional shape, we thanked the driver for the thrilling experience. "You could make a killing as a driver's education instructor in LA," I told him. He seemed amused. We weren't. We parted company with the agent and inched our way to the hotel. I don't think I drove faster than ten kilometers an hour the entire way.

I assumed that my mom and sister would want to spend the remainder of the day resting or making sure my mother's teeth were glued back into her mouth, but apparently the pull of shopping was too powerful to resist. By noon we were in a cab on our way to the shopping district of Lisbon. As compelling as our early-morning driving lesson was, we decided it best to leave our rental car at the hotel. When we parked it, black smoke was still seeping from under the hood, and two of the four hubcaps were missing. The car looked as though it should be jacked up on concrete blocks in someone's backyard. No wonder the rental company was called Last Resort.

CHAPTER 4

Smoldering Credit Card Plastic

I t didn't take long for me to recall that I was traveling with two of the most formidable shoppers in the civilized world. My mother first drew attention in the early 1960s when she was old enough to shop on her own. Merchants in her hometown would call her at home if she hadn't been in for a few days. She's won customer of the year at no less than a dozen major retailers, and it was rumored that twice the United States government seriously considered naming an economic stimulus plan after her.

When I was a child, my mother would take my siblings and me to Kmart so she could chase blue light specials. She claimed it was good exercise. We all knew it was an addiction. Lisa, on the other hand, had far less experience but was by no means a slouch. By the time our plane landed, she had already mastered the following phrases in Portuguese:

You can go lower than that.
I didn't fly all this way for a twenty percent discount.

*Please don't make me come behind the counter. Do you know
how hard it is get bloodstains out of a polyester blend?*

I'm amazed how Lisa could nearly flunk math in high school yet
tell you precisely how much you could save on an item if you waited
for it to go on sale and used a triple coupon.

As soon as the taxi dropped us off at the entrance to the shopping
district, it was evident my mother and Lisa had already been sucked
into a foggy haze of sale signs and heated haggling. My mother
hurried over to an empty bench and laid out a map of the city.

"Okay, this area is known for shoes," she informed Lisa as she
circled a spot on the map.

My sister leaned in. "I think this is where we can get leather
bags," Lisa said as she pointed to another section of the map.

My mother nodded excitedly. "And here are the two best public
restrooms."

---

*Side note: I'm still shocked that the Department of
Homeland Security never recruited my mom and
sister. Their map had more Xs and arrows on it than
Joan Rivers's face prior to a Botox treatment.*

"You two are like serious detectives," I said as I watched them
mark up the map and debate about their plan of attack. My mother
looked flattered by the comment. And just as quickly as they had
mapped out their strategy, they were gone.

A few hours later, I arrived at the café where we had agreed to
rendezvous. I walked through the café a few times, but didn't see
either of them. I made my way back to the entrance to see if they
had grabbed a table outside. That's when I noticed my sister through
the front window. She was leaning back in her chair with a wet
towel draped over her forehead, wearing an expression on her face
that suggested she had just barely outrun a pack of wild dogs. My

mother was hunched over the table, rubbing her bare feet against the pavement. I exited the restaurant and approached their table.

"What are you doing?" I asked my mom.

"Trying to get rid of blisters." She remained hunched over while I rounded the table and took a seat next to my sister.

"How did you know we were out here?" Lisa asked.

"I followed the scent of smoldering credit card plastic." My sister smirked. I looked down at the two small bags lying on the ground under the table. "This can't be all you bought." Without looking up, my mother pointed to an area behind where we were sitting. At least a dozen bags of varying sizes were piled on top of one another. "Oh!" I said. "We might have to take the *QE II* home to haul all of this stuff."

My mother looked up. "Is that possible?"

I remained silent.

We ordered some food and spent the next hour sharing stories of the afternoon's activities. I probably didn't need to hear about how my sister flashed dozens of passersby as she tried on camisoles being sold by a sidewalk vendor. I asked my mom if she got any pictures of the people's faces. She stared at me as if she had just received terrible news.

"Oh, my God!" she shouted. "My camera! I forgot to bring my camera today."

Lisa and I knew this was serious. If there was an activity my mother loved more than shopping, it was taking pictures. I thought a camera flash was raising me for the first ten years of my life. Whenever I called out for my mother, a flash would appear. "Didn't want to miss the moment," I'd hear from behind the blinding light. Looking back, I thought it was strange to hear my mother say "Hold that pose" or "Look this way, sweetie" after I fell off my bike or jumped too high on our neighbor's trampoline and landed in a thistle bush in the next yard. Even when I thought I had total privacy, I'd often hear the faint click of a shutter. I know it's hard to believe, but if you flip through all of my mother's picture books, you can see a large portion of my childhood play out before your eyes.

"I'm sure there will be plenty of opportunities for pictures," Lisa said. The comment didn't help, because my mother looked defeated. She wore a look that told us she had a specific picture goal that was now in serious jeopardy. The previous year on a weekend trip to upstate New York my mother snapped eleven hundred pictures. We thought we might have to take her to the emergency room for radiation exposure. For the Portugal trip she brought a digital camera with two memory cards that held three thousand pictures each, and she purchased a traditional camera with twenty rolls of film. That's roughly four hundred pictures per day, and day one was almost over.

"When we get back to the hotel, I want to take some pictures of the lobby," my mother said. Her request wasn't as strange as it seemed. Despite taking an exorbitant number of pictures, only a small percentage of the pictures my mom took were actually of anything we'd recognize when we returned home. She has catalogues in her attic filled with pictures of blurry-faced strangers, doorjambs, the inside of her pocket and purse, people's feet, the toiletries from her hotel room, and street signs.

Later that evening we found ourselves on the shared balcony between our two rooms. We decided to order room service and spend the remainder of the evening sipping wine and catching up.

Side note: Well, Lisa sipped Diet Coke while my mom and I hovered next to the minibar like a couple of teenagers waiting outside a liquor store.

"I had fun today," I told them.

"Me, too," my mom replied. My sister had just taken a bite of her sandwich, so she nodded enthusiastically rather than risk choking while attempting to speak her affirmation, despite the fact that she was sitting with two Heimlich specialists.

My mom placed her head on my shoulder. "I just wanted to say thank you for this trip," she said. "It's really generous of you." I felt a surge of guilt. I didn't have the heart to tell her that the only reason we were sitting on that balcony while sipping wine and enjoying the scenic landscape of western Portugal was because I had convinced myself I was dying of ass cancer.

"It's the least I can do for torturing you for most of my childhood," I said.

"And early adulthood," my mom added. We both laughed because we knew it was true.

I wanted to stay focused on the whole guilt thing, but a surge of nostalgia came over me. "Well, actually this trip is not happening because of something I did to you," I told her. "It's something you did for me. For us."

My mom sat up. "What did I do?" My mom wasn't fishing for compliments; she sounded sincerely humble.

"You gave us the best childhood anyone could have asked for," I said. I hate to admit it, but I can be a softy when it's absolutely necessary. Lisa put her napkin down and placed her hand on my mom's leg.

"He's right. We had a blast growing up. You made it a lot of fun."

I drifted off for a moment as I remembered those early years. The sound of my mom chuckling at Lisa's stories stirred me back into the conversation. Lisa and I took turns sharing memories of our childhood. Lisa recalled the movie nights when our entire family would dress in pajamas and my mom would pass out candy corn. Then there were the trips to the beach, where my mom would help us find seashells and we'd make fun of the older ladies who wore swimming caps and ugly, one-piece bathing suits. I reminded my mom of the birthday cakes she used to make for us in the shape of cartoon characters or zoo animals.

"Do you remember when I made you the Ms. Pac-Man cake," my mom said to Lisa.

"Yeah, you put boobs on it."

"How else would you know it was Ms. Pac-Man?"

Lisa raised her eyebrows. "Lipstick and eyelashes?"

"Oh," my mom whispered.

Lisa and I giggled for a while as we reflected on those years. We certainly did have a lot of fun. Then my mother asked a question that neither my sister nor I expected.

"Did you both really enjoy your childhoods? I mean, you said earlier that you had great childhoods. Is that true?"

"Absolutely," Lisa answered. I emphatically agreed as I leaned in and put my arm around my mom.

"We could give you a million more examples of how much fun we had, but what we most appreciate is how you made us feel," I told her. "We always felt like we were home."

My mother placed her head on my shoulder. Then she gently took my sister's hand. I kissed my mom on her forehead and then stood up to pour myself another glass of wine.

"Oh, can you refresh mine, too?" my mom asked.

As I walked back to the table I noticed my mom wiping her eyes with her napkin. I filled her glass and sat next to her.

"I am so happy to hear you say those things," my mom told us. "I tried my best to make sure you had the childhood I never had."

Lisa and I exchanged looks. My mother rarely talked about her childhood. It was a mystery to everyone in our family. She occasionally made vague references to living with her father for several years before she was a teenager and then venturing off to nursing school at the age of nineteen, but that was about it. I knew my mom didn't come from privilege or significant means. She ran a lean household, making do with secondhand clothes and subsidized school lunches, and we didn't have much in the way of luxuries. But we didn't want much either. My mom kept the family engaged through conversation, games, and laughter. She didn't need to rely on the gimmicks that other parents in our neighborhood were forced to use to keep their children from planning a coup, such as expensive toys and designer clothes.

"What was your childhood like?" I asked.

My mom laughed uncomfortably. "I've had way too much chardonnay to start talking about my childhood. Maybe some other time."

Lisa and I didn't push her. Instead, we sat next to her and shared in the enjoyment of the beautiful views of the city from our balcony. I knew some families could communicate through silence, but ours wasn't one of those families. *We were a speaking family*, I thought. I had to say something. I knew my mother expected it.

"You okay?"

She looked up at me and smiled. "Yeah."

We sat together for another several minutes before we called it a night. I felt grateful and sincerely happy for those few hours we spent together on the balcony, and I hoped I'd have another opportunity for that kind of time with them again. Spending time with my mom really did feel like home.

CHAPTER 5

Not So Silent Hill

The next day we decided to carve some time out to visit a short list of churches and museums we had read about in a Lisbon travel guide my mom had purchased at our hotel. We spent the better part of the morning touring a church where archaeologists had recently discovered the foundation of an ancient city. Much of the churchyard was dug up, and we were restricted from entering a few areas of the church's interior because of the ongoing excavation. We had a lovely conversation with the groundskeeper, whose job it was to tend to the church's gardens and educate visitors on the church's history and the role it played in the city's lengthy past.

After a brief monologue highlighting several key milestones related to the church, the groundskeeper asked us to guess when we thought the church was built. We were terrible at this type of game. The typical American's knowledge of world history didn't go much beyond 1620. We knew the church was old, but we had no comparison. When Americans are asked to think of something ancient, our reference point is Betty White.

"Well, let's see," I said. "The church is made of stone, and stone was popular during which time period?"

"The Stone Age," Lisa replied with a hint of sarcasm.

After a rather awkward debate amongst our team, we threw out a guess of sometime between when Noah built his ark and when the *Titanic* sank. I was fairly sure we were correct, but the groundskeeper didn't have the sense of humor that was required to enjoy our company, so we were forced to move on with our tour. I hate to admit it, but that conversation with the groundskeeper reinforced the nearly ubiquitous stereotype across Europe of the ignorant American.

We spent the early afternoon touring a handful of museums that distinguished themselves by offering exhibits that rivaled those at better-known museums in other parts of Europe. To be honest, I don't recall much of what we saw. The only thing I remember from that afternoon was the hill on which I nearly brought my sister to tears. Let me explain. The "hill" was a steep incline that stretched four city blocks and was the only barrier separating us from a neighborhood known for its port wine. When we arrived at the base of the hill, I looked up the street and concluded that it didn't appear to be very formidable but would certainly pose a challenge. My sister, always on the lookout for the easiest solution, noticed a trolley station nearby.

"Do you think the trolley is running today?" she asked.

"It looks like they're closed," I replied.

My mom walked over to the ticket window. "How can they be closed on a Saturday?"

I stood with my hands on my hips as I contemplated our options. "I guess we'll take a stab at walking," I said. I knew there'd be pushback, especially from Ms. Pragmatic.

"Just for the record, I'm opposed to this," Lisa said. "It's hotter than hell, and that's a big hill."

My mom scanned the streets behind us. "Can't we just get a cab?"

That seemed like a good idea, but there weren't any cabs in sight. We waited several more minutes to see if a cab might drive by, but none came. I decided to take things into my own hands and offered a bribe.

"If you both agree to walk up the hill with me, I'll buy dinner tonight."

My mother and sister were sophisticated hagglers. "At a restaurant of our choice?" Lisa asked.

"Including drinks?" my mom added.

I nodded in agreement to both, and before I knew it, we were headed up the hill. We had walked about a block when I stopped and looked back.

"This doesn't seem so bad."

"Speak for yourself," my mom said, huffing and puffing. "Is it just me or does the top of the hill look like it's getting farther away?"

My sister stopped and leaned over to catch her breath. "It's not just you. It feels like we're walking in place."

I walked back to them. "Stop being so dramatic. It's not that bad."

My sister straightened and looked back down the hill. "We should have waited to see if the trolley opened."

"The trolley isn't operating today," I replied. "Let it go."

"We've made it this far, so we might as well keep going," my mom said. We walked another block or two. This time my mother stopped and sat on a bench outside a closed bakery. "Jesus," she said as she tried to catch her breath. "I'm afraid to look up the hill. Are we any closer?"

"I can't see anything," Lisa replied. "There's sweat running into my eyes."

"We're almost there," I said. My mom stood up and stretched her legs.

"You told us that fifteen minutes ago." She removed her outer shirt and tied it around her waist.

"I think I'm dehydrated," Lisa said.

I rolled my eyes. "Already?"

"Have you noticed there's no one else on this hill?" asked Lisa. "And all of the stores are closed. There's not even a place to get water."

I am so over this, I thought, but I needed to keep the momentum going. I jogged in place and flapped my arms. "Let's keep going. We're almost there."

My mother and sister reluctantly followed me. The slope of the hill quickly increased, and we found ourselves using everything from street signs and lamp posts to bike racks to pull ourselves forward. Even I became winded.

"I have to stop for a minute," my mom said. "This is insane." She slowly lowered herself onto the curb. My sister's face was the color of Sheetrock, and her body language suggested that she, too, might drop to the ground at any moment. "My quads are seizing up," she informed us.

"It's good for you," I replied. "Just think, we'll all have buns of steel by the time we get to the top."

"If I wanted buns of steel, I would have bought the damn DVD," my sister said. "And what good will steel buns be when I'm on a respirator in some Portuguese hospital?"

My mom looked up. "I'd kill for a respirator right now."

My sister dug through her purse and pulled out a handful of hard candies. She unwrapped one and popped it into her mouth. She handed one to my mom and me. "Here, this will help fight off starvation and dehydration." As she returned the candies to her purse, a few coins fell out onto the ground.

"I'd pick those up," my mom said. "We'll need them for my hip replacement." My mom started to get up and then sat back down.

"I'm not sure I can continue. I haven't exerted myself this much since I popped out your brother, Jeffrey. He was a breach baby, you know."

My sister had obviously been looking for an opportunity to remind me that this walk was my idea. "Great. Now we've got an elderly woman who's clearly in compromised health."

"Hey, I'm not elderly. I'm fifty-seven."

My sister looked apologetic. "You know what I meant. Elderlyish." Lisa's response didn't appease my mom.

"I didn't drag the two of you up here," I replied. "And besides, you both know that if there was a shoe sale at the end of this walk the two of you would have torn up this hill like a pair of Olympic sprinters." My sister's body language quickly shifted from "on the verge of dying" to "I'm gonna knock some sense into you."

"And secondly—" I began before I was interrupted. Lisa removed her sunglasses and handed them to my mother. Then she pounced on me. *Holy crap!* I thought as we rolled down the sidewalk together. "For someone complaining of sore thighs, you sure have a strong grip," I said.

"Well, you wouldn't be in this mess if you had listened to me and waited for the trolley to open," she said, barely able to catch her breath.

I was officially irritated. "The trolley is not running today!" I shouted. She squeezed her legs tighter. "Jesus! What are you, a boa constrictor?"

"How the hell do you know the trolley isn't open? We didn't even wait long enough to find out." We rolled farther down the sidewalk.

"THE TROLLEY IS NOT RUNNING!" I yelled, almost losing my voice. That's just about the time I heard it.

Ding. Ding.

Ding. Ding.

We stopped rolling and looked up to see the trolley slowly

climbing the hill. To make things worse, the trolley was jammed full of people, all pressed against the windows, hoping to catch a glimpse of my sister in the process of severing me in half with her death grip.

Side note: How the hell was I supposed to know the trolley was running? My mom and sister were the ones who had the marked-up map and claimed to be detectives. You'd think that would have been an easy problem to solve.

We stayed on the ground, frozen in embarrassment, as we watched the trolley pass us, then stop a few yards away to pick up our mom. Without hesitation, she pulled herself onto the trolley and waved good-bye to us. "See you at the top," she mouthed as the trolley released its brake and continued up the hill.

Lisa said, "I'd consider finishing you off right now, but the thought of watching you squirm for the next few days is worth keeping you around."

"Just for the record, I've been lying here for the past ten minutes with your ass cheeks pinning me down, and I have to say they feel like steel to me. I think a thank you is in order." Just when I thought she couldn't squeeze harder, she clamped down. I groaned. "Okay. That was an important organ."

It took us another twenty minutes to reach the summit. When we arrived, we found our mother sitting at an outdoor café, her feet resting on an empty chair and a cold glass of chardonnay in her hand. "You must be absolutely reveling in this," I said.

My mom lowered her sunglasses and looked at us over the rims. "You have no idea."

Lisa collapsed into a chair. "Thanks for bailing on us, Mom."

My mom waved the waiter over. "Well, the two of you seemed so intensely preoccupied with your couples therapy, I didn't want to interrupt."

"Funny," I replied as I, too, took a seat. We didn't intend to spend more than an hour or so at the café, but we literally couldn't move. I went through three ice packs, and my sister drank four liters of water. My mother and I decided to rehydrate using God's elixir: fermented grapes. We discussed taking a walk through the neighborhood, but none of us could recall why we wanted to come there in the first place. Somewhere on that hill we had lost our memory. Our short-term memory loss was all the motivation we needed to stay put. By the time we gained enough strength to get up, the café had already closed. We mustered up the initiative to hail a cab, and within an hour we were back at the hotel, preparing for what would turn out to be our biggest adventure yet.

CHAPTER 6

Twelve Inch a Slave

The next day, we set off on a side trip to a region of southern Portugal called the Algarve. Based on the directions I printed at the hotel, the trip should take just under four hours. I planned on five to six hours because I had learned to overestimate due to my inability to navigate. More than a few people have told me that it was a miracle I was born naturally and didn't require rescuing from my mother's womb via a C-section. Even now, if you spin me around two or three times in my driveway, I'll probably surrender to the grip of a panic attack before someone is able to lead me back to the house.

At about the four-hour mark I knew something wasn't quite right. What gave it away were the frequent stops we were forced to make to allow flocks of waddling birds to cross the dirt road we found ourselves on.

"Are those chickens?" Lisa asked at one point as we slowly rolled past a small flock of fowl.

My mother looked up from her crossword puzzle. "They look more like geese."

"I think we're slightly off track," I said.

"I thought you had a map," my sister said from the backseat.

"I do have a map," I replied. "But clearly the map is not accurate."

"Oh, a typical man!" my mom said. "Blame it on the map." I pulled the car over to the shoulder. "Everyone knows you have no navigation skills, so just admit we're lost."

We're definitely lost, I thought. It was clear we were no longer on a highway, but there was no way I was giving my mom the satisfaction of seeing me admit she was right. "We're not lost! The roads in this part of the country are obviously underdeveloped."

"Underdeveloped?" my mother replied. "Wild animals are crossing the road."

"I wouldn't exactly call a few birds wild animals. I had the worst timing, because just as I said that a large flock of wild turkeys slowly moved into the road in front of our car. I raised my open hand in front of my mother's face in anticipation of her opening her mouth. "Don't. Just focus on your crossword puzzle." She remained quiet for a few moments while she pretended to be engaged with her puzzle. But, as expected, she chimed back in.

"What's a four-letter word for *can't find way?*" she asked as she tried to hold back a smile.

I elected to take a few moments to focus on deep breathing and connecting with my core rather than thoughts of homicide, which was a technique I had learned in Saturday Catholic school.

"This would be a lot less stressful if you weren't adding commentary, Mother."

"Okay, you're right. I'll be good." She shot my sister a look that implied *Help me out, please.*

"Are we going to die tonight?" Lisa asked. "It would be a shame to think we survived that driving lesson in Lisbon only to bite it on a deserted road in the middle of nowhere."

"We're not going to die," I responded. "And we're not in the middle of nowhere. I know exactly where we are."

"Where exactly are we?" my mom asked.

"Portugal." My mother raised her eyebrows, prompting me to elaborate. "Southern Portugal," I added with an inflection in my voice that made it clear even I was uncertain.

"You have no idea where we are, do you?" Lisa said. I shifted uncomfortably in my seat. "Why don't you let me navigate," she added. "I'm good at this stuff."

"Well, it's getting dark, so someone should take control," my mom said.

I looked around a few times, dropped my head, and took a few more deep breaths. "I can handle this. I think we just need to turn around and take that road we passed a few hundred yards back."

I knew I needed to perform a three-point turn in order to turn the car around, and I immediately understood why fifteen years earlier that pudgy state police officer requested I successfully perform one during my driver's test. He saw this day coming. The first point of the turn went by without incident. The second point in the turn is when things got a bit sketchy. As we backed up, the car headed toward an old wooden split rail fence. Darkness was fast approaching, so my depth perception was thrown off a bit. Well, that's the excuse I used, anyway. I thought I had plenty of space to back up to make room for one last turn. I was wrong. The car bumped the fence with a moderate amount of force. I stopped the car and looked over my shoulder. My sister was sitting up, looking out the back window.

"I think you hit the fence," she said. I'm sure she was trying to be helpful, but it was a perfect moment to fine-tune my sarcasm.

"You think so?"

"You might want to scoot forward," my mother told me.

"Oh, really? I thought I might just continue backing up to see what else we could run over. Apparently I hadn't finished fine-tuning my craft."

"I'm just trying to be helpful."

"I told you I could handle this." I gently pressed the gas pedal. I didn't realize I was still in Reverse. The car jerked backward, and I immediately heard a loud crunching sound coming from underneath the car. Several moments of uncomfortable silence passed.

"Oops," my sister said. I wanted to release the death grip I had on the steering wheel and jump into the backseat to show her who was boss, but as I quickly reflected on the countless other times she and I had tussled over the years I came to the unfortunate conclusion that I'd likely emerge the loser.

"Drive forward, please," my mother said with a tone that suggested she was embarrassed for me.

Side note: Why the hell was I the one driving? Everyone, including my driver's education coach, knew I had no navigation skills. I would have loved to be the one in the passenger seat shouting out crossword clues as I watched someone else run over wild turkeys and wooden fences.

I placed the car in Drive and inched forward. For a good five seconds the only sounds we heard were those of fence posts falling to the ground and breaking apart like brittle twigs. I stopped the car because I was afraid I might do more damage to the fence.

"That was quite a turn," said Lisa. "That driving lesson earlier this week really paid off."

I glared at her in the rearview mirror. "Don't you have some candy to choke on back there?"

"Honey, I think your IBS is kicking in," my mom said. She had plenty of opportunity to ease into the argument, but she opted to go straight for my Achilles heel. During my adolescence I spent more hours than I care to admit sitting in the office of any gastroenterologist who was patient enough to listen to me go on and on about how I was convinced I was dying of colon, stomach, esophageal, throat, or any of the other cancers of the digestive system. Most of the doctors were a good sport and sat quietly as I regurgitated (no pun intended) all of the evidence I had gathered from medical books at my town's public library. My eventual diagnosis was an "emotional colon," more commonly known as IBS—irritable bowel syndrome. Needless to say, this diagnosis was welcome fodder for my family.

"What have I done to deserve the two of you?" I asked. "I'm a nice person. I try to live my life in a generous, kind way, and what do I get in return?" I placed the car in Park. "Sarcasm, drama, and judgment."

My mom turned to face my sister. "I think he hit his head when he knocked the fence over." My sister nodded. "Sweetie, I think you're experiencing some memory loss. Since the time you were a baby, you've been the gold standard for sarcasm and drama. For Christ's sake, you have an excitable colon. How much more dramatic can you get?"

"It's an emotional colon," I whispered in return.

I looked to my sister for help. I didn't get it. "Drawwwma," she whispered slowly as she overannunciated both syllables and held up her open hand while my mother replied with an emphatic high five.

"I give up," I said. "The two of you are on a mission to send me plunging over the edge into the depths of insanity. You win!"

"That wasn't dramatic at all," my sister said under her breath.

My mom reached for the door handle. "Let me get out to direct you."

"No, Mom, I can handle this," I replied, but she had already exited the car and was headed toward the fence.

"This should be interesting," Lisa said as she opened a bag of Twizzlers. I suppose she expected a riveting comedy to unfold on the side of that country road.

"Okay, back up twelve inches," my mom yelled from behind the car. I looked back to make sure I could see her. It wasn't difficult to make her out. Even though it was dark, I could see her waving her arms to signal me to back up. I placed the car in Reverse and slowly backed up. "Keep coming!" my mom yelled. I felt I had backed up way farther than I had room for, so I slammed my foot onto the brake pedal. "Why did you stop?" she screamed.

"I thought that was twelve inches," I yelled back.

"What measurement system are you using?" she shouted. "The same one men use to measure their penises?" My sister giggled.

"Get in the car," I yelled. "You're angering the only child you have who is likely to take care of you when you're old and crapping the bed."

"I'm not angry," Lisa informed me.

I slowly turned my head and looked over my shoulder. "Really?"

My mother reluctantly got back into the car, and we eventually completed what had to be the world's longest turnaround. We felt bad about the damage we caused to the fence, so I tacked a handwritten note to it. The note contained a brief apology and our contact information.

Side note: Well, okay, that's not true. I actually wrote the following on the piece of paper: I'm sorry about the fence. Two crazy women are holding me against my will, and I damaged it in my attempt to escape. The ringleader has silver hair and chardonnay breath. Heading south. Please send help.

CHAPTER 7

The Lavender Yeti

With the car turned around, I drove back to the road we had missed, and after another two hours we eventually got to Lagos, the small walled village where we planned to stay for a few nights. When we arrived at the hotel, we parked the rental car and went to the check-in desk. We noticed the clerk from halfway across the lobby. He had a smile that literally filled his whole face, much like The Joker.

"Welcome!" he said. "We're happy to have you." We thanked him for the warm welcome.

"Where are you traveling from?" he asked.

"Lisbon," I replied.

"Oh, what did you think of the new highway?"

I looked at my sister and Mom in confusion. "New highway?"

The clerk stopped what he was doing and looked at me. "Yes, a new highway just opened last month connecting Lisbon and the Algarve." It shaves almost two hours off the trip."

I leaned on the counter and placed my head in my hands. There are moments in my life when I see beauty all around me while there are other moments when I want to drop to my hands and knees and pound my head against the ground until my brains spill out. Listening to the hotel clerk fell into the latter bucket.

"Would you do me a favor? Would you take that letter opener you're holding and jam it into the side of my head a few times?"

"Are you okay, sir?"

Side note: Did he really think I would ask to be stabbed with a sharp instrument if I was okay?

I wasn't okay. I had just spent four hours more than I should have in a beat-up rental car with two people who I was convinced wanted me to suffer. I wanted nothing more than to be immediately directed to the hotel's prayer room or the nearest private nook so I could lose my mind without drawing too much attention. That didn't happen. Instead, I slumped over the counter and repeatedly banged my head against it.

My mom stepped forward and used the moment as an opportunity to showcase her improvisation skills. She told the clerk that I had been recently released from a mental institution after having spent three years receiving therapy for believing that I had a pet platypus named Pat. She asked the clerk to tread carefully as Pat had been known to influence me to do bad things.

The clerk looked at me with fear and curiosity. Without hesitation, I played the role my mother had assigned me. I had learned years earlier that it was far easier to just go along with my mom at such times. I looked directly at the clerk and laughed awkwardly. I then buried my head in my mother's chest and sobbed while I called out Pat's name. My mother kissed the top of my head and gently nudged me toward my sister. "Well, you're off to a good start," my mother told the clerk as she dramatically gathered our check-in paperwork.

I overheard the clerk tell my mother he could have a rollaway bed placed in her room rather than taking the risk of having me alone in my own room. My mother's response was classic. "Oh, that's not necessary," she said. "We tie him to his bed at night." I never got a good look at the clerk after my mother's response, but I could imagine beads of sweat rolling down his forehead. "But you could send a bottle of chilled chardonnay to my room. Consider it a gesture of sympathy for what I've had to endure for the past ten minutes." The clerk nodded nervously.

"You're some piece of work," I told her as we walked to the elevator.

"You'll be thanking me soon. Everyone in this hotel will be falling all over each other to make sure you're happy. No one wants you to snap."

"Real funny. How would you feel if everyone thought you were nuts?"

"Uh, look at who you're talking to," Lisa said.

I looked at my mother and immediately understood my sister's point. My mother was wearing a sweat suit that was obviously a size too small and white sneakers that were obviously a size too big, and her hair could easily be mistaken for one of those big gray hornet's nests that you might find hanging from a tree branch.

"Don't make fun of your mother," she told us. "Bad things will happen."

"Wasn't today bad enough?" I asked.

"Today?" she replied. "That was just a warm-up."

The elevator door opened on our floor. "Everybody happy now?" my mom asked.

"Happy as an unpredictable psycho on a weekend pass," I responded. My mom chuckled, not because she thought I was funny but rather because she knew she had set the stage for a potentially interesting stay at the hotel. She was serious about that afternoon being nothing more than a warm-up. We reached my room first. I opened the door and walked inside.

"Hey, psycho, we'll be back in a few minutes to tie you down," Lisa said to me. I contorted my face and stuck out my tongue as I closed the door behind me. I felt bad for the clerk because I was sure he didn't sleep a wink that night and instead thought about all the ways I could escape my room and cause havoc throughout the hotel with Pat. The havoc never materialized because I feel asleep as soon as my head hit the pillow. The havoc would have to wait until morning.

Early the next day, we met at the elevator. We planned to eat breakfast together in the hotel's restaurant before we set out for a day of exploring.

"Really, Mom?" I said. "The lavender sweat suit again?"

My mom looked down at her outfit. "What? I always buy multiples."

"I'd love to see you in a navy blue or gray pantsuit."

"Well, then get me a job as a flight attendant."

"You're afraid of flying," Lisa said. "I think that might be a dealbreaker." My mother conceded.

The elevator stopped at the next floor. Two elderly Portuguese women entered. Both were dressed in light blue-and-white housedresses that looked like traditional maid uniforms. I also noticed they both wore circulation socks and clunky black shoes. Each woman was holding a saucer and tiny teacup brimming with hot tea. When they entered the elevator, they quickly turned around to face the door. My mother, who was the shorter of us three, was at least a foot taller than the two women. One of the women turned around and made eye contact with my mom.

The woman was clearly startled, perhaps intimidated by the

lavender yeti standing behind her, and she immediately turned back to face the door. She looked at her companion and then bowed her head. Her hands shook violently, causing her teacup to rattle loudly against the saucer.

"She must think she's on the menu this morning," I whispered to my mother.

The elevator stopped on the first floor, and before the door had completely opened the two women rushed out of the elevator. They were in such a hurry to get away from us that they tripped over each other, and one of the women's shoes flew off and remained in the elevator as the door closed. Of course we were concerned about the two women, but we couldn't help but laugh all the way to the ground floor. We intended to turn in the shoe to the hotel's lost and found, but my mother decided to hold on to it for a while longer. For the remainder of the morning, each time a tiny Portuguese tourist walked by, my mother held the shoe up to her mouth and said "Mmmmm. Tastes like chicken." She can be so cruel.

CHAPTER 8

Badass Sea Bass

The next day, my mother and sister decided to head into town to shop the afternoon away. I hated shopping and was quite content to wander through the streets and people-watch. I found Lagos to be quite pleasant. It was a quaint, seaside fishing village with narrow cobblestone streets and sand-colored homes made of stone and rock. Because the town was far removed from Lisbon, not many locals spoke English. My mom and sister had little trouble communicating because everyone speaks the language of money. I, however, have never been able to pick up foreign languages. I took French classes for fifteen years and still can't say more than a few sentences. Six years ago while taking private French lessons I decided to invest my time in learning the most likely sentence I would need to use. I'm now fairly proficient in saying *A quel commissariat de police avez-vous porté ma mère?* Loosely translated that means, "Which police station did you take my mother to?"

On my walk I stumbled upon a small, waterfront café that caught my attention. The front door was open, and I could hear cheers and chanting coming from inside. I was intrigued, so I stepped inside. A crowd of about forty people stood around a small table in the back of the café. Sitting at the table were an old, weathered-looking Portuguese woman and a middle-aged Portuguese man. On the table were several empty espresso cups. It became clear that the elderly woman and middle-aged man were involved in some type of drinking contest, each being required to slam shots of espresso until the other quit or passed out. At that time I was an avid coffee drinker and could easily consume three or four espressos in a single day (and you wonder why I have an emotional colon). I wanted in on this contest.

Side note: My competitive nature has resulted in some awkward situations over the years such as the time I blew out my neighbor's knee playing flag football (I didn't know she was autistic) or when I completely obliterated my five-year-old nephew at Chutes and Ladders. No one told me there was an age when you were supposed to let people younger than you win to help boost their confidence. Wouldn't it be better to just tell them that not everyone can be a winner and call it a day?

After a few awkward conversations with the café staff, in which I tried to piece together the three Portuguese words I knew to ask about getting into the contest, I found myself sitting at the table across from the elderly woman. I don't recall what became of the man who had sat in the seat before me. All I knew was that it was my turn to take on the old lady. From what I could gather, she was the longtime reigning champion, and no one had come close to beating her. She sat quietly and stared at me with her dark, beady eyes. I stared back as best I could and tried not to blink, assuming that blinking might be perceived as a sign of weakness.

My tactic didn't last long. I don't know if she had two glass eyes or had super lubricated eye sockets, but the woman never blinked. I had to. As soon as my eyelids reopened, the woman picked up her espresso and drank it in one gulp. The crowd remained eerily silent. I picked up my espresso, swigged it, and slammed the empty cup onto the table. "Game on," I said. A few of the people gasped while others whispered to one another.

"I come from the land of Starbucks and Dunkin' Donuts," I told her. "You're doomed." I knew she had absolutely no idea what I was saying, but I felt it gave me an edge. The woman's body language made it obvious she was not impressed. *This woman is unreal*, I thought. *Is she a robot?* I tried a different tactic, one that was a bit more direct. "I'm sure you're a nice lady, but you're going down like Anna Nicole Smith on a rich centenarian." Still nothing.

A moment later the woman lifted the second espresso and drank it. I did the same. This back and forth went on until we reached the fifth espresso. At that point I became worried. The old lady didn't seem to be affected at all by the caffeine. I was already extremely jittery, and my heart felt like it was about to jump out of my chest. She, on the other hand, looked as though she might nod off at any moment. My concern grew with each second that passed because I wasn't sure I could drink another espresso.

Thank God I didn't have to. Not only did the lady look as though she was going to fall asleep, she did. As she reached for the fifth espresso, she leaned forward, placed her head on the table, and began to snore. I looked at the crowd, they looked at the lady, and before I knew it I had a beer in my hand and was lifted out of my seat by a few of the people standing near me. They all cheered and shouted. You would've thought I had just killed the wicked witch and by doing so I liberated the entire town.

The crowd carried me outside, where I was rewarded with my prize: a whole sea bass. *What the hell?* I thought. This was a first for me. The fish was cold and slippery. I assumed it had been sitting on ice during the contest. I had no idea what I would do with a whole sea bass, but it looked badass, and I was elated and proud as hell.

"*Obrigado!*" I shouted to the crowd. "Thank you, thank you!"

As I attempted to lift the sea bass over my head to get the crowd more riled up, I became dizzy, and my stick-figure legs began to buckle. The shots of espresso had kicked in. The next thing I knew I was lying on a stretcher with an oxygen mask strapped to my face. Two EMTs carried me along the waterfront as if I was Cleopatra being paraded through the streets of Alexandria. Humiliation doesn't even begin to describe what I felt. I was literally thirty seconds away from ripping the mask from my face and jumping off the stretcher when I heard my mother's voice.

"Stop!" she screamed as she ran over to us.

I was so glad to see her and my sister. Through the mask I said, "Thank God you're here. Can you tell them I'm fine?"

My mother approached the two men who were holding the stretcher. "Would you mind lowering the stretcher so I can get a picture of all this?" Without hesitation, the men lowered me into the scope of my mother's camera lens. "Honey, can you turn this way? I want to make sure I get the fish in the picture."

I don't think my mother realizes to this day how lucky she was that I had that frozen sea bass pinning my arms down.

Costa Rica (2004)

CHAPTER 9

Three Powdered Doughnuts

Several years had passed since our trip to Portugal, and I had finally forgiven my mother for leaving me on that stretcher while she and my sister took pictures and ordered gelato for themselves and the two EMTs. My mother had the nerve to order pistachio, my favorite. Okay, maybe I haven't quite forgiven her yet. Anyway, Pete and I hadn't seen my mother for several months, so we were delighted she accepted our invitation to join us on a holiday to Costa Rica. Pete and I had heard great things about Costa Rica, so we were really amped about the trip. My mother arrived at our house the evening before we were to depart. The next morning, we set out for the airport. When we arrived at Boston Logan airport, we parked the car and headed toward the departures concourse.

"Does everyone have their passport?" my mother asked.

"I have mine," I said.

Pete took his passport out of his front pocket and held it up. "Do you have yours?"

My mother stopped and dropped her bag onto the floor. "Oh, boy! Stop, please," she said frantically. "I have to dig it out of my bag."

We waited a few minutes as my mother emptied her overstuffed carry-on. Out came the lipstick, tissues, bags of candy, paperback romance novels, Sudoku puzzles, sunglasses, one of those egg-shaped callous removers, a backgammon board game, jewelry, a knitting kit, a lint roller, and countless other health and beauty items.

"Are you moving to Costa Rica?" I asked.

She continued digging through her bag. "You won't be giving me a hard time when you need one of these things."

"We're staying at a legit hotel," I said. "We're not taking you on *Survivor*, Costa Rica edition."

My mother's face was still buried in the bag. "Got it!" she cried with both surprise and relief in her voice. My mom shoved all of her personal belongings back into the bag, and we continued on toward the check-in desk. My mom has always been a fan of casual clothing, and she often went out of her way to dress comfortably. For this particular trip she once again sported her go-to outfit, the lavender sweat suit and white sneakers.

"How do I look?" my mother asked.

My mom is by no means heavy, but she does have a bit of junk in the trunk and under the hood, and on this particular occasion she had a bit stuffed in the glove compartment. Given the lavender sweat suit and big purse, I just blurted out the first thing that came to mind. "Like the gay Teletubby." My mother smiled faintly as she drew an imaginary circle around me with her right pointer finger.

"Is this going to be your attitude the entire trip?"

Side note: It was 5:30 A.M., I was caffeine deprived, and she knew I was relatively gifted with sarcasm. What was she expecting me to say, that she looked like Cindy Crawford?

58

"People demand honesty, but God forbid you give it to them," I said as I yawned.

Pete put his hand on my mother's shoulder to comfort her. "I have to admit I can see the gay Teletubby, but I think we look more like the unsuspecting stars of an awkward family photo. Did we get dressed in the dark?"

Pete and I were wearing matching tan plaid shorts, heavily wrinkled polo shirts, and flip-flops. My mother laughed. "Actually, you look like guests on *Jerry Springer*. Aren't there laws against this in your community?"

"What did you expect us to be wearing?" I asked. "Seersucker suits and bowties?"

"Yes!"

She had a point. For gay men, we fell well short of the general public's expectation of us in terms of our attire. But it was way too early in the morning for me to stress over it. We approached the self-service kiosk and began the process of printing our plane tickets. My tickets came out first, then my mother's, and then… silence. Pete's tickets didn't show up. We stared at the machine for several minutes, hoping it would start up again and spit out Pete's tickets, but we soon concluded that a different solution would be needed.

"What do you think? Pete asked me. I shrugged.

"Should I rock it back and forth?"

"I'd kick it."

Of course neither of us thought of calling an agent over. This debate went on for a good five minutes before my mother walked up to the machine, positioned her legs wide apart for what appeared to be stable footing, swung her overstuffed carry-on as if she was a Bulgarian Olympic hammer throw champion, and clouted the machine's right side. The kiosk's screen flickered for a few moments, and then out popped Pete's tickets.

"Wow!" I cried. "I want to hit it now to see if I can get an upgrade voucher."

My mother shot me a cold stare. "Laughing at my bag now?"

Pete simply couldn't witness the pummeling of an innocent ticket kiosk, so he walked away as I pounded the machine with one of my flip-flops behind the wide stance of the gay Teletubby. I was surprised Pete didn't stick around, as he is the person I turn to when I need to get stuff done. He is rarely intimidated and has nerves of steal. He's also the person our friends call in the middle of a blizzard when all of the liquor stores within a twenty-mile radius are closed, because they know he has a stash of vodka in the basement.

When Pete tells the story, he claims he saw my mother put the kiosk in a wrestling hold. I don't remember that, but I do recall helping my mother climb atop the kiosk as if she planned to ride it like a mechanical bull. Pete should have been horrified at this sight, but I think he found pleasure in watching the two of us work together to solve a problem. He smiled and silently encouraged us.

In addition to being a vodka hoarder, Pete is a pilot, air traffic controller, event planner, human resources expert, and a military serviceman. Or more simply put, a classic overachiever.

"We should give you a superhero name," I said as I high-fived my mom.

"How about Svetlana Idranktoomuch," Pete yelled from across the concourse.

My mother glowered at him. "Careful, Pete. I have knitting needles."

We didn't get that upgrade voucher, but my mother and I had enjoyed ourselves as we worked out some preflight jitters, so it was a good use of our time.

Two bottles of champagne later we landed in the capital city of San Jose, survived the agonizing wait going through customs, and decided to grab a taxi and explore the city center while we waited for our connecting flight at the municipal airport across town. As we headed for the airport exit, we were excited to step outside into the warm Costa Rica sunshine. It was early April, and the weather back in New England was still chilly and damp. We all agreed that some warm sun would be good for our soul.

"We're finally here!" my mom cried. "I can't wait to get outside." We pushed our way through the heavy revolving door at baggage claim and stepped out onto the sidewalk. The next few moments are still a little fuzzy, but I do recall my mother dropping her carry-on and taking a huge breath through her nose. This turned out to be a bad idea. Within the span of a few seconds my mother was hunched over, grasping her chest, barely able to speak.

"Hot...b-b-urn!" she said as she stomped her right foot. The temperature had to be at least 110 degrees, and the humidity was thick enough to slice. My mother had basically taken a huge breath of invisible fire. "Jesus Christ!" she screeched. "There should be a sign on that revolving door warning people to hold their breath until they get into a cab."

"I know. It's really hot," Pete said.

My mother moaned as she straightened up. "Hot? I've cooked dinner in ovens that were cooler." Pete walked over to my mom and rubbed her back. "How do you feel?"

"Like I just inhaled cheesecake."

"That shouldn't feel strange to you," I said.

My mother took a few steps closer to me while she wiped sweat from her forehead with her sleeve. "Remember the kiosk back in Boston? I still have another swing in me."

I backed off. I found great pleasure in teasing my mom, but even I knew I should hold off until she was able to take a full breath. Besides, she was far more fun when she was able to fight back.

Out of necessity we quickly jumped into a taxi. The three of us crammed into the backseat and asked the driver to drop us off downtown. We soon noticed that the taxi had no seatbelts, air conditioning, a meter, or back windows. As we pulled on to the main road, my mother, who was sitting in the center seat, leaned forward and placed her hands on the ledge that separated the front and back seats. "Do you have to hit all of the potholes?" she asked the driver. The question wasn't surprising to me. Costa Rica was home to some of the world's worst roads, and many of the potholes were so large they had names and appeared on the more credible road maps.

"I'm sorry, ma'am," the driver responded. "They're hard to avoid."

Pete leaned forward. "Is there any good stretch of pavement around here?"

"Your plane landed on it," the driver said. That reply sort of killed the conversation.

We continued to downtown San Jose in relative silence. Because of the poor road quality, the cars kicked up a considerable amount of dust and dirt. Since the taxi lacked back windows, by the time the driver pulled up to the main square to drop us off we were covered in a thick layer of white dust. The driver turned around to collect the fare from me and immediately began to chuckle when he saw us.

"What?" I asked.

"You look like three powdered doughnuts back there."

My mother grabbed his shoulder. "I hate to break it to you, amigo, but you don't look so hot yourself."

The driver looked at himself in the rearview mirror and nodded. He, too, was covered in dust. He looked like the Grim Reaper, so we were glad the ride was over. We exited the taxi, dusted ourselves off, and sat down at an outdoor café. We were anxious to dig into some of the local cuisine, so we poured over the menu with intense scrutiny. Eating while traveling has always been tricky for me, especially since I found out I have an emotional colon. I wanted to try the local fare, but I feared I might spend the rest of the vacation tossing my cookies or, as my mother referred to it, "praying to the porcelain goddess."

When the waitress came over to take our order, Pete went first. "I'll take the burger, please, and make it well done. Oh, and add a basket of fries."

My mother rolled her eyes. "Well, that's adventurous." She looked at her menu. "We're in Central America. Live a little." My mother lowered her menu and looked at the waitress. "I'll take the grilled cheese."

"Really?" Pete said, and slapped his forehead.

"With a side of the house salsa," my mom added and then glared back at Pete. Then everyone's gaze shifted to me. I felt an incredible amount of pressure. I scanned the menu, looking for something exotic but colon-friendly like crispy tarantula sliders or a capybara mac and cheese, but the food seemed awfully familiar. America's love of fast food favorites had already forged its way toward the equator.

"I'll take the chicken sandwich. No fries."

"Wow, that was brave," my mom whispered to Pete. I cringed.

The two of them chuckled. Clearly, bravery was not in the cards for us at that café. Little did we know that we were reserving our nerves of steel for our second plane ride of the day.

CHAPTER 10

Xena: Warrior Princess

We arrived at the municipal airport and stepped up to the ticket counter to check in for our flight from San Jose to Quepos, a small village in the southwest corner of Costa Rica. Quepos was home to the airport closest to Manuel Antonio National Park, where our hotel was located. The airline agent asked each of us to step onto a scale so he could record our weight and properly balance the plane.

My mother stepped forward reluctantly. "What do you mean balance the plane? Could it tip over?"

The agent laughed. "It won't even get off the ground if it's not properly balanced."

Paranoia muted the glimmer in my mother's eyes. "Well, can't you just use an estimate based on your best guess?"

"No, ma'am. We need your accurate weight."

"Okay, okay," she said. "I'm one-forty plus tax and tip."

The agent didn't acknowledge my mother's attempt at getting a laugh. "Ma'am, can you please step on the scale?"

My mom hesitated at first but agreed to be weighed if she could have a few minutes alone in the restroom. She dropped her carry-on bag onto the floor, took a few items out of it, and walked toward the restrooms. About fifteen minutes went by before Pete and I noticed her. I couldn't believe my eyes. My mother had removed her lavender sweat suit as well as her jewelry and white sneakers. She wore a makeshift skirt and a halter top that looked as though it was made from an old sheet. She stood in the doorway of the restroom for a few moments, confident, stoic, and barefoot.

"Mom! We're going to a national park, not auditions for the remake of *Xena: Warrior Princess*," I said, still in disbelief. She walked past me toward the scale.

"Don't start with me right now."

"I think she's wearing paper towels," Pete said. He didn't have it in him to stick around to watch the scene that was about to play out at the weigh-in station, so he walked outside, where our tiny plane was waiting. My mom stepped onto the scale. The agent looked at the reading and then opened his mouth to shout my mother's weight to his coworker, who was positioned on the other side of the terminal.

"One—" he said before my mother interrupted. Well, it wasn't really an interruption as much as it was an ambush. My mother used her position on top of the raised scale to lean heavily on the agent's right shoulder.

"Sweetie, don't even think of shouting that number across this terminal," she whispered. "I'm a highly anxious grandmother who's running low on Xanax. And in case you haven't noticed, I'm wearing paper towels." The agent stared at her blankly. "In America, we refer to this as being on the brink," she added. "Do you get the general drift of what I'm telling you?"

The agent froze for a moment and then quietly nodded as my mother stepped off the scale.

"Atta boy," my mother said as she winked and walked toward the restroom, where she changed back into her sweat suit.

I walked outside. Our plane was what you might refer to as a puddle jumper. It had about ten seats and a large propeller in the front. I recall the propeller because it took the pilot three attempts to get it to start spinning. If the engine hadn't started on the fourth attempt, I planned on walking to Quepos. When my mom finally joined us, she immediately focused on the plane.

"Please tell me we are not getting into that tin can," she said. "I thought you told me we were connecting on a regional jet."

"Well, I didn't want to upset you," Pete replied. "Besides, this plane is totally safe."

My mother didn't look reassured. I wasn't convinced, either, but I felt I needed to at least try to reassure my mom.

"Mom, Pete is an accomplished pilot, and he wouldn't get on, or advise us to get on, an unsafe plane. This will be a lot of fun. Trust me."

Side note: There really should be an acting award for best improvisational performance while crapping one's pants. I can already envision my acceptance speech: And lastly, I'd like to thank my mom. It was her brilliant episode of paranoia on that tarmac in Costs Rica that gave me this opportunity to shine.

"Is there beverage service on the flight?" she asked, hoping for an outlet for her anxiety.

Pete pulled three single-serving bottles of white wine from his backpack. "Of course."

"Thank God!" she replied.

After we boarded, an especially young-looking man in a uniform boarded the plane and jumped into the pilot's seat.

"Please tell me it's take-your-child-to-work day," my mother said.

"I think that's the pilot," Pete told her.

"Isn't there a requirement to have graduated puberty to be a pilot?" she asked. I have to admit, the pilot didn't look a day older than thirteen.

"Not always," Pete said.

I looked at the pilot. "I think he's carrying a teddy bear."

"You're not helping," my mom whispered as she glared at me.

A few minutes later, the young man turned around, introduced himself as the captain, and asked if we had any questions about the flight. None of the other three passengers was paying much attention, but my mother quickly raised her hand.

"Is your father joining us?"

The pilot laughed. "No, ma'am. I'll be taking this one on all by myself. It's actually my first solo flight." We all hoped he was joking. My mother gripped my arm and shouted, "Technically, it's not a solo flight if we're on it."

The pilot laughed louder. "Well, I'm sure you'll all be fine. Just sit back, relax, and enjoy the hour flight to Quepos."

"This is going to be the longest hour of my life," my mother said. "When does beverage service start?"

Pete reached into his backpack and handed her a bottle of wine.

"He just placed the teddy bear in the co-pilot seat," I said.

"You do that to age me, don't you?" she asked. "Just for that, I'm drinking your wine."

"Don't even think about it. Just because you're a ball of nerves doesn't mean I have to suffer."

The pilot completed his preflight check, and soon we rolled down the runway and lifted off.

"Uh-oh, the teddy bear just fell out of the co-pilot seat," Pete said. My mother closed her eyes tightly.

"Is the kid still seated?" Pete leaned into the aisle and looked toward the front of the plane.

"Yup."

"Keep your eyes on him," she said.

About twenty minutes into the flight, the pilot turned to face the passengers and announced that we'd soon be passing over Arenal, the country's largest active volcano.

"Did I hear him correctly?" my mother asked Pete. "A volcano? With lava and ash?"

"Yes, you heard correctly."

Pete was rarely interested in getting sucked into the unrealistic fear my mother and I had regarding air travel. He tried his best to placate us when possible, but he definitely had a limit.

"The chance of the volcano erupting and spitting up a column of fiery lava and ash high enough to affect our flight is quite low," he added.

"How low?"

"There's a greater likelihood that our plane will unexpectedly break apart in midair and send us all plummeting toward the earth to our death."

Apparently, he had reached his limit.

"I don't like you right now," she told him. She turned to me for comfort, but of course I, too, was flirting with the edge of a nervous breakdown. At that very moment we hit a patch of moderate turbulence, which my mother and I used to fuel our paranoia.

"Mom, in case the plane does break apart and we fall to our death I wanted to let you know that I apologize for torturing you during my childhood." I took her hands in mine. "I know how much stress I caused you, and for that I'm truly sorry." I hugged her.

"That's the biggest crock of shit I've ever heard. You derive a great deal of pleasure torturing me. And I hold you partly, if not mainly, responsible for turning me into the ball of nerves I am today."

I held back a smile. "I see this conversation is going nowhere."

Right then the plane hit another patch of turbulence, causing it to shake and tilt momentarily. There was a sense of urgency on my mother's face. She pulled a Xanax out of her purse and downed it with a swig of her chardonnay.

"We're going to die!" she cried. "Well, I suppose now is as good a time as any to tell you that I'm sorry for threatening you with an exorcism. I felt it was the only way to get you back on track, but I can see how that may have adversely affected your self-image, your masculinity, and perhaps even your sexuality. I'm deeply sorry for that. I just wanted to share that with you before we crashed."

"I'm not giving you my wine."

She laughed. "You started this game. I was just going along to make you feel better."

"You are a new kind of evil. Do you know that?"

"What have I ever done to you?"

My mind was immediately filled with thousands of examples of the "things" my mother had done to me over the years. I wasn't sure where to begin. "Are you kidding me?"

She looked at me as if she had absolutely no recollection of the previous thirty-four years. "Give me an example."

"How about the time you secretly dressed up like a mummy and crashed my Halloween party during my freshman year of college."

"So?"

"You beat me in beer pong and watched me kiss Brian Dougherty. And I wasn't even out yet."

"That's right! That's the night you wore the nun habit. What was your name again?"

I looked at her with complete contempt because I was absolutely confident she recalled the name; she just wanted to hear me say it out loud. "Sister Mary Catherine Zeta Jones," I muttered.

"Yes, of course! By the way, you still owe me a magnum of chardonnay for my win." She took a big gulp of wine straight from the bottle. "And for the record, I knew you were gay then."

"You did?"

"Well, your costume that night sort of confirmed it, but what really gave it away was the double rainbow that came flying out of me when you were born and lit up the delivery room like the aurora borealis."

"Oh, kind of like Sookie," I said.

"Who?"

I rolled my eyes. "Sookie Stackhouse from *True Blood*. She's half human and half faery, and she's able to generate a powerful light that's used to fight evil spirits and to heal people."

My mom gaped at me as if I were speaking Mandarin Chinese. "Can you come back to reality for a minute, please?"

"Listen," she said. "I know you think I behave badly, but you and I are a lot alike, and we're not bad people. We're interesting, and people often confuse interesting with bad." She raised her half-empty wine bottle in salute. "There's nothing worse than being around a boring person, believe me. There's a responsibility that comes with being interesting, and I'm hoping to see you rise to the occasion. Boring is easy. Interesting takes some initiative." She winked at me and then downed the rest of her chardonnay.

Pete, who had moved his seat while my mom and I chatted so he could keep an eye on the pilot, stood up and approached. "Whatcha talking about?"

"My mom is giving me a performance review," I replied. Pete shook his head and retreated to his seat. He knew all too well that when my mother and I got on a roll, we would be looking for someone to torment. He was smart to back off. In the few remaining minutes before we landed I sat back and stared at my mom. I sincerely enjoyed spending time with her. I knew a lot of people who never had a chance to get to know their mother, and I felt incredibly lucky that my mom enjoyed spending time with Pete and me. Don't get me wrong. Sometimes I wanted to strangle her, but mostly our time together was filled with fun and excitement and a level of honesty I found liberating.

CHAPTER 11

Crouching Grandma, Hidden Dragon

Luckily, our plane landed safely and on schedule in Quepos. The airport there was a single landing strip carved out of a banana plantation. There was no formal terminal. Instead, passengers huddled under the roof of a small hut to get out of the sun or rain. On the tarmac my mom congratulated the pilot and wished him well with the remainder of his adolescence. Within minutes, we had retrieved our bags, flagged a taxi, and were on our way to the hotel.

Once in our hotel suite we stepped out onto the private terrace and took in the scenery. In the short time we sat on the terrace we saw an abundance of wildlife—hummingbirds, turkey vultures, pelicans, brown-footed boobies, iguanas, and at least two hundred geckos of varying size and color.

Pete pointed to a citrus tree on our far left. "Look! There's a toucan."

"Let me get my camera!" my mom cried as she jumped up and ran into the suite.

Pete leaned over the terrace wall. "Whaaaa! Whaaaa!"

"What the hell are you doing?"

"I'm trying to draw the bird closer."

"That's supposed to help? You sound like a wounded water buffalo. The poor thing is probably terrified." My mother had returned, camera in hand, and tried to capture a picture of the bird.

"Oh, man, it's too far away."

"Don't worry, Pete's trying to call it over using some bizarre bird call."

"You have a better idea?" asked Pete.

My mom's face lit up. "Wait! I have an idea." She ran back into the suite and returned with a small box of cereal from the minibar. "Here," she said as she handed the box to Pete.

"Fruit Loops?" Pete asked.

"Look what's on the front cover," she said. "A toucan!" We laughed at this discovery. My mom opened the box of cereal and threw a few pieces toward the bird. I could tell she was still too far away. To get closer she dropped to the terrace floor and crawled toward the far end.

"Look! It's crouching grandma, hidden dragon," Pete shouted. All three of us laughed.

Still on her hands and knees, she scuttled to the far end of the terrace and attempted to stand up. "Oh, crap! I'm stuck," she said as she looked up, wincing.

"What do you mean you're stuck?" I asked.

"It's my bum knee. I'm not twenty-two anymore, you know."

Pete and I had a choice to make. We could help my mother back onto her feet or we could have some fun. We chose fun.

"Let's open a bottle of wine," Pete said.

When the cork popped, my mom said, "Oh, man, is that the buttery chardonnay we brought with us?"

"Uh-huh," I replied.

"You're going to leave your mother on her hands and knees while you enjoy a refreshing beverage? In this heat?"

"For a few minutes, yes," I replied. "Tell you what. We'll help you up if you sing us a song."

"A song? Are you kidding me?"

Pete took a sip of the wine. "Mmmm, this is so good."

"Which song?" she asked.

"I'm thinking a show tune," I said to Pete. "What do you think?"

"No, I'd go with something cool like a dance hit." I could tell my mother's patience was running out.

"Oh," I said. "How about 'Who Let the Dogs Out?'"

"Ooh. That's a good one," said Pete.

Side note: She sort of had this coming to her. She should never have left me lying on the sidewalk in Lisbon while my sister squeezed me down to a size twenty-six waist.

My mother shifted back and forth. "I hate you!"

"I'm just putting some initiative into being interesting." She stared at me, and I couldn't tell from her facial expression whether she was boiling mad or proud that I had taken her advice. Either way it was a small victory for me.

"My arms are going to give out soon," she said. "And my back is seizing up." Pete and I ignored her attempts to get out of her current situation. After about ten seconds, she opened her mouth and sang, "Who let the dogs out?" It was terribly off key.

"Don't forget the barking," Pete said. "We'd like to see you really get into it."

"He's totally corrupted you, hasn't he?" she asked.

"We're waiting," Pete replied.

My mother stared at Pete as if to send him a clear message that she wouldn't forget this. "Woof, woof, woof, woof," she barked. "Can you help me up now, please?"

Pete and I applauded and then helped her up. She headed directly for the wine. When we finally calmed down, we realized we were laughing so hard the toucan had flown away. The bird probably came to the same conclusion that any other living creature arrives at after meeting us, and it had escaped when it had the chance.

CHAPTER 12

Knock, Knock!
Hoo-Hoo's There?

The next day, we decided to spend some time at the hotel's pool. My mom ordered a drink and immediately submerged herself in the heated water. Pete and I weren't quite ready for a swim, so we decided to take a walk to explore the hotel property. As we walked away about a dozen guys entered the pool area. We decided to stick around to conduct some light reconnaissance of the group. By overhearing bits and pieces of their conversations, we determined that they were friends from Alabama and were in Costa Rica to do some fishing. The men appeared to be in their forties and fifties, and several had tattoos on their arms and neck. I couldn't tell for sure, but it looked like all of the men were smoking cigarettes.

"Should we stay with your mom?" asked Pete.

"Maybe for a few minutes." I wasn't trying to stereotype, but the group did look intimidating. We strolled back to the pool and sat on the edge of the shallow end and dipped our feet into the water. My mother waded over to us and rested her drink on the edge of the pool. "Don't trust me to be alone?"

"No," we replied simultaneously. My mother rolled her eyes dramatically.

This is when one of the fishermen jumped into the pool and made his way to us.

"Howdy, y'all," he shouted. As the man approached, I noticed he looked significantly younger than his friends. His cropped salt-and-pepper hair was misleading because his face offered little evidence of aging. He was tall and lean and was wearing white board shorts with large blue lilies printed on one side, and his aviator sunglasses were pushed high up onto his forehead. We politely returned his greeting. "Where y'all from?"

"The deeply liberal northeast U.S.," I responded. I always felt the need to make it crystal clear we were bleeding-heart liberals.

"Oh, okay," he said, laughing. "I'm Jim. I'm from Alabama. I'm here with my buddies on a fishing trip." He pointed to the group of guys who were hovering around the outdoor bar. He reached out to give me a fist pump. I had never seen a fist-pump greeting before, so I extended my hand and shook his fist. That handshake will likely make the list of my most awkward moments. I'm sure he thought, *Typical liberal.*

"Sounds like a lot of fun," I said, still feeling humiliated.

"So who is this lovely woman?"

Pete and I looked around curiously.

"I think he's referring to me," said my mother.

"Oh, sorry," I replied. "This is my mother, Alta." They shook hands and engaged in small talk. Pete nudged me to indicate that he wanted to take that walk around the hotel property now. I nodded, but I wanted to make sure I set the right tone with Jim.

"Excuse me, Jim." He looked up at me. "My partner and I are

going for a walk now, and I want to make sure you understand that if she gets into any trouble, I will hold you personally responsible."

He laughed. "Okay."

"I'm dead serious," I continued. "First, she's married. Second, she's only been out of jail for a few months, and she still shows signs of the homicidal tendencies that landed her there in the first place. That reminds me, Mom, did you take your medication yet today?" Jim's eyes widened. "Don't be the guy who pushes her back over the edge. The last guy to do that didn't fare so well."

"He's pulling your leg," my mother assured him. Jim didn't look convinced. As Pete and I walked away from the pool, I turned around and made a hand gesture at Jim that implied *I'll be watching you.* I truly hoped the lies I had told Jim would be enough to scare him into keeping my mother out of trouble while we were gone.

After our walk, Pete and I found ourselves at the indoor bar overlooking the pool area. An hour had expired since we left my mom with the fishermen. We were engrossed in a conversation with the bartender, who was from Panama, when Pete looked over my shoulder.

"What is it?" I asked.

"Uh, I think I just saw your mom being tossed into the air."

"What?" I cried. Pete and I rushed to the window. Soon the bartender joined us.

Sure enough, my mom was in the pool—drink in hand—while four of the fishermen tossed her into the air in what looked like some white-trash Cirque du Soleil performance. They were chanting. "Alta! Alta! Alta!"

"She looks like she's having fun," the bartender said.

"This is not about her right now," I replied. "Think about how this is impacting me."

"Maybe you just need to relax a bit," he said. "You're on holiday."

"Oh, yeah, nothing says relaxation like seeing your sixty-year-old mother holding a scorpion bowl and being tossed into the air by a bunch of tattooed fishermen."

"And she's in a one-piece," Pete added.

Side note: I take complete responsibility for the one-piece. I should have been a better son and advised her against it. The polka dots made her look like a Twister mat. It's obvious to me now the fishermen weren't tossing her into the air for fun; they were trying to toss her back to her room.

"Good point," replied the bartender as he walked back behind the bar. "What's your plan to get her back to her room?"

"Oh, that's easy," I replied. "We'll just shoot her with a tranquilizer dart from our balcony. Once she's asleep, we'll go retrieve her."

"It's kind of like relocating a stray bear," Pete added.

"If she suddenly slumps over, you'll know why," I informed him.

He chuckled. "I'll keep an eye out for that."

We decided it best to leave her be for a bit longer. She did seem to be having fun, and the fishermen appeared harmless. Pete and I finished our drink and continued our walk around the hotel grounds. A few hours later, we returned to the suite to see if my mom was ready to go to dinner. When we walked into her room, she was lying in bed under the covers.

I shook her leg to wake her up. "Mom. Get up. It's time for dinner." She moved a bit but otherwise didn't respond. I shook her leg again, harder this time. "Mom. Get up. We're hungry."

She lifted her head slowly. "Okay, give me a second."

I backed up and stood beside Pete as my mother rolled out of the bed and stood up. She stretched her arms above her head and yawned. I forgot to mention that she was also completely naked. I froze. I honestly didn't know what to make of this.

"Why is it so dark in here?" she asked.

"You have eyeshades on," I replied. I don't know how I actually spoke those words, because every muscle in my body had seized up.

My mother lifted her eyeshades and grabbed the alarm clock off the nightstand. "How long was I out for?" she asked, totally oblivious that a) she was naked and b) our jaws were resting on the floor. I coughed softly in an attempt to get her attention. My strategy worked. My mother looked down and then raised her gaze slowly to meet ours. "Oh, boy," she said calmly. I closed my eyes and nodded in affirmation. "Let me fix this," she said. She snatched a cocktail napkin from the table outside the bathroom and slapped it against her left shoulder.

Pete whispered to me, "That wasn't even close."

"I have a feeling she wasn't aiming for anything."

"She couldn't have used her pillow instead?"

It was more of a rhetorical question. I stood quietly for a moment and then decided to take matters into my own hands.

"Mom," I tried to say. I think the sheer shock of the situation had dried my mouth out. I tried again. "Hi, there," I said calmly. "Pete and I appreciate your effort to conceal yourself behind that extremely small cocktail napkin, but you might want to shift it a bit south, if you get my drift." She looked down. "There's a far more important area just below the equator that you might want to consider covering." She looked at me for a few seconds as if she was attempting to parse what I had just shared with her. "Remember the double rainbow?" I asked. Her facial expression seemed to indicate that she understood what I was telling her.

"Oh, I see. I'm embarrassing you. I'm going to the bathroom to get ready for dinner." With that, she turned away from us and walked toward the bathroom. As she approached the bathroom door, she repositioned the napkin to the center of her lower back and then closed the door behind her.

"That was payback for yesterday. I'm sure of it," I said.

"Uh-huh."

Several minutes passed before either of us said another word.

"I just saw your mother's hoo-hoo," Pete said as his voice cracked.

I stared blankly at the bathroom door. "I don't mean to diminish the trauma you're experiencing, but *I* just saw my mother's hoo-hoo."

"Well, in my defense you've seen it once before."

"Yeah, okay. But that was thirty-four years ago, and my eyes were glued shut. I now have tonight's vision seared into my retinas. When I blink rapidly, all I can see is an ill-positioned cocktail napkin and a—"

"Double rainbow."

"Yeah, something like that."

Side note: Seeing my mother attempt to conceal herself with a three-by-three-inch cocktail napkin is the kind of shit that keeps therapists employed.

We left my mother's bedroom and walked into the foyer, where we waited for her to join us. A few minutes later, my mom emerged from the bathroom dressed for dinner. None of us mentioned a single thing, and instead we headed out the door. We decided to walk to the restaurant. It was already quite dark, and the roads were not in great condition, but the restaurant was only a quarter mile away, so we thought we'd be safe. I tend to walk faster than most people, so I was roughly fifteen feet ahead of Pete and my mom. A few minutes into the walk, Pete dropped back a few feet, and that's when I heard the scream. It was my mother. As she screamed, I looked back to see her white sneakers clearing the guardrail.

Pete leaned over the railing. "Alta!"

"Mom! Are you okay?" I shouted, too, as I leaned over the guardrail. My mother was on her back about a foot below the edge of the road in what appeared to be a rain gutter. She tried to stand up.

"Do you need help?" Pete asked.

"No, I'm fine. I'm just down here enjoying the smell of this honeysuckle I noticed." Pete and I looked at each other, confused. "Of course I need help!" she cried. "Get me the hell out of here."

Pete pulled her out of the gutter and lifted her back over the guardrail onto the road. It was so dark that we couldn't see what condition she was in.

"I can't see anything," Pete said as he brushed debris off my mom's back.

"Why don't you have Sookie over here shine some light on us," my mom said as she glared at me. At precisely that moment I turned on my iPhone, which generated just enough light to assess my mom's condition. Pete and my mom looked at each other with surprise at my perfect timing. Thankfully, my mom was relatively unharmed. One of the straps of her tank top was torn loose, and there was a small tear in her jeans at the right knee.

"I don't know how this happened," she said.

"They named a drink after you at the pool," I replied. "Do you think that had anything to do with it?"

My mother seemed pleasantly surprised. "They named a drink after me?"

Side note: I just want to clear the air. My mother doesn't actually drink that much, but I think it's fair to say that she can't handle scorpion bowls or any drink with the suffix tini.

I took a deep breath and debated whether I should hug her tight or put her back into the gutter. Pete jumped between us and gave her a huge hug. I thought he picked the wrong choice, but that's just me. We remained quiet for the remainder of the walk. I was glad she wasn't hurt, but she definitely needed some assistance at the restaurant to get her clothes back in order. When we arrived at the restaurant, I approached the host.

"Hi," I said. "We just found this woman on the side of the road. I think she fell, and it looks like she might need some assistance with her clothing."

"Oh, my," he said as he took my mother's arm to support her.

I whispered to the host, "I also think she's a little crazy. She keeps claiming I'm her son." The host nodded and led Mom into a room off the reception area. When he returned, we let him in on our prank. Initially he thought we were two lunatics, but after a little persuasion, he agreed to go along with the plan.

Pete and I grabbed a table and ordered some appetizers and drinks. About thirty minutes later my mom emerged from the back room and crossed to our table.

"Wow! Did they curl your hair?" I asked. She stood next to our table, arms crossed and silent.

"Your teeth look whitened," Pete said.

She did look a bit fresher than when we left her with the host. Clearly the time she had spent in that back room was to her benefit, so I was happy for her.

"I'm so mad at you two right now," she said loudly. The host turned and looked at us. "I can't believe you told them you found me on the side of the road. And that I was crazy?" She nudged me aside, sat down next to me, and grabbed a nacho from the plate in the center of the table. "Me? Crazy?" she continued, her mouth half full. "I was alone and scared in that room while the two of you were out here sipping wine and enjoying yourselves." As she made this last comment, a young woman who worked at the restaurant approached our table.

"Hi, ma'am. Here are your purchases from the gift store." The woman handed my mother a large bag.

I raised my eyebrows. "Gift store?"

My mother lifted the glass of wine we had ordered for her and took a sip. "Well, it was right next to the reception area, and they had the cutest refrigerator magnets. They even had ones with toucans on them! Besides, you pawned me off on total strangers. What did you expect me to do?"

We were silent for what seemed like an eternity, and then simultaneously we burst into laughter, the type of laughter that engages every bone and muscle in your body. Pete and I jumped up and gave my mother a big hug and kissed her a dozen times on each cheek. We spent the rest of the evening laughing and recounting the day's events. My mom really didn't know they had named a drink after her at the hotel, so she was excited about trying it the next day. She asked us the name of the drink, but we couldn't remember it. Pete thought it was "One-piece wonder," and I thought it had something to do with Alabama. It wasn't until the next day that we learned the drink was named "Grandma-tini," which of course explained everything.

When we arrived back at the hotel, Pete decided to go to bed early because he wanted to be rested for our excursion the next morning. My mom and I weren't quite ready to go to bed, so we headed to the terrace. One of the amazing things about being in a remote area is the degree of darkness at night. The sky was full of stars, far more than what we were accustomed to seeing, having spent most of our life in the suburbs.

"Wow!" my mom whispered. "Look at that sky."

"I know. I've never seen so many stars before. And it looks like it's a full moon, too."

My mom stood near the terrace wall, where she could see the twinkling ocean beneath us. She waved me over. "It's like three hundred and sixty degrees of stars," she said as she looked out across the Pacific.

"Do you ever wonder what's out there?" I asked as I looked up. My mom kept her gaze on the water below.

"I have a hard enough time trying to make sense of what's happening down here." She rubbed my back for a moment and then walked back to the padded bench and sat down. I followed. We sat quietly for several minutes as each of us watched a series of shooting stars race across the sky and fade into the horizon.

"What are you thinking about?" I asked. I regretted the question as soon as I asked it because I hated when someone asked me that question. It's a question people ask when they feel uncomfortable with the silence. My mother had to be annoyed with the question as well, but she was kind enough to respond.

"I'm thinking about how beautiful it is here. And how my preconceptions have been completely demolished."

"What do you mean?"

"I don't know. I think I had a somewhat naïve perception of the culture here before we arrived."

I knew what she meant. Americans don't get many opportunities to learn about the culture of other countries. We tend to rely on the mainstream media to educate us.

"Were you expecting to see Sally Struthers standing in a mud puddle with impoverished children running around behind her?"

My mom laughed. "Not exactly, but I certainly wasn't expecting the stunning landscape and the genuinely kind people. Everyone here seems content."

"Are you content?" I asked her.

She said immediately, "Sure," then stopped herself. "Yeah, I guess I am. I mean, no one's life is perfect, but they can certainly still be happy."

She looked at me. "Are you happy?"

I didn't see that coming. "Yeah, although I don't really have anything to compare it to."

My mom sat up and reached past me to grab a blanket that was draped over the arm of the bench. "Sure you do. You told me you were really happy when you were a kid."

"True," but aren't all kids basically happy?" My mom unfolded the blanket and spread it across her lap. "Weren't you happy when you were a kid?"

"There were times when I was happy, but it was mostly a struggle."

I slipped my sneakers off and placed my legs on the coffee table in front of us. "I still don't know much about your childhood."

"It's not my childhood you should be asking about. My twenties were far more scandalous."

"Well, start talking."

"I was sort of joking. Besides, I'd be giving you way too much material to use against me."

My mother was keenly aware I had a tendency to poke fun whenever I could. She was wise to steer clear of revealing too much at that point. Despite the risk of me collecting valuable ammunition, my mom did share a few stories that night about her adolescence. She wasn't as rebellious as I had once assumed. The more she shared, the more I realized she and I were a lot alike. Her conversation with me on the plane the previous day made sense to me now. We both used humor to mask insecurities and vulnerabilities that we were afraid others would see. It was our camouflage.

As I watched my mom talk, I noticed for the first time the subtle lines around her eyes. I had never really thought about my mother aging. I guess it's something children don't think about until they find themselves changing a bedpan. It didn't matter to me. If you could look beyond the lavender sweat suit and crazy hair, she was the most beautiful person in the world.

"I'm glad we're here," I said. "Here on this balcony tonight and here in terms of where we are in our lives."

"Me, too."

We didn't stay out on the terrace much longer, but I wish we had. Watching the moonlight flicker across the ocean was mesmerizing, and it felt like the perfect end to an adventurous first day in Costa Rica. "I love you," I told her.

"I love you, too. But if you think I've forgotten about the stunt you pulled at the restaurant tonight, you're kidding yourself." She tapped her head with her fingers. "I'm tucking that one away."

My face became hot, mostly out of nervousness. "But I *really* love you," I said in a lame attempt at charming her.

She stood up and walked toward the terrace door. "Nice try, but I'm going to get even. You do understand that, right?"

I laughed nervously and nodded. I had lived thirty-four years, and the one thing I was certain of was that my mother was going to get even. She had probably begun to plot her next move already. I was condemned to sit back and wait.

"Good night," she whispered and walked into the suite.

My stomach clenched. *I'm totally screwed.*

CHAPTER 13

To All the Girls I've Loved Before

The next morning we joined a small tour that was organized by the concierge at our hotel and traveled by bus to Manuel Antonio National Park. The park was well known for its sizeable population of three-toed sloths and white-faced monkeys. When we arrived at the park, we exited the bus and followed our tour guide toward the forest. At the edge of the forest, the tour guide stopped. He smiled and said, "My three goals today are to make sure you learn something about the rain forest, to keep you safe, and to make sure you have fun."

We all nodded in agreement.

"To keep you safe, it's important that I take a moment to draw your attention to the most serious risk here in the park."

Unsolicited, members of our group offered answers. "Dehydration," yelled one person. Another said, "Spiders?"

"Good answers, but not the right one," the guide said. "The biggest risk you will face in the park is the possibility of encountering one of the many venomous snakes that reside here."

Our tour group collectively gasped.

"Poisonous snakes?" Pete cried. "Oh, hell no."

I knew that Pete had an intense phobia of snakes, so I wasn't surprised that he began to show signs of complete mental collapse. Whenever Pete thinks there's a snake nearby, his ability to think and behave rationally becomes moderately impaired. I planned to remain optimistic, but I didn't have high hopes for how that tour would play out.

Side note: One time on a vacation in Florida, Pete saw a small garter snake in the courtyard of our hotel and spent the next hour warning the elderly couple in the room next to us about the "legless" creature just outside their door. He went so far as to tell them, "I simply can't identify with things that don't have legs." Imagine our shock when we discovered that the husband was a double amputee.

"There's no such thing as a poisonous snake," the tour guide added. "Snakes can be venomous but not poisonous."

"That's semantics," replied Pete.

"The snakes won't bother you if you don't startle them," the guide explained in an attempt to calm Pete, who was now pacing back and forth, clenching his fists.

"What if I startle one accidentally?" asked Pete. The guide lifted a big stick that he'd been carrying.

"That's why I carry this big stick. I'll shoo it away." The tour guide went on to tell us that he took the same approach as one of our presidents, Teddy Roosevelt, who said, "Walk softly and carry a big stick." I was embarrassed after hearing this piece of U.S. history because my mother had taught my siblings and me that Teddy Roosevelt's foreign policy was to "walk purposefully and carry a reliable wine opener."

"Shoo it away?" Pete muttered. "You're not reassuring me. Don't snakes chase you?"

"Not usually," the guide said. "Just stick with me, and you'll be fine."

I looked at my mother and knew immediately that she wouldn't let this opportunity pass.

As we trekked through the forest, she shared vivid stories of the deadly black mamba of Africa. One story was about a documentary she had seen in which an entire South African family was chased down and attacked by the highly aggressive snake. She pulled her knitting needles out of her bag to show the group the size of its fangs. From that point on, Pete heard rattling coming from every corner of the park. I don't think his feet were on the ground for more than ten seconds at a time for the remainder of the tour.

About halfway through the day we entered a dense and dark part of the rain forest, where we could barely see five feet in front of us. As we turned down a narrow dirt path to move deeper into the forest, a loud roar echoed overhead.

My mom clutched my arm. "What the hell was that?"

"It's probably a poisonous tree snake," I replied. "I mean venomous."

Pete froze.

"It sounded more like a T-Rex," she said. "I knew I should have paid more attention during *Jurassic Park*."

The tour guide turned around. "It's not a T-Rex or a venomous snake. That sound came from a howler monkey, the largest primate in the Americas."

"I always thought your father was the largest primate in America," my mother whispered.

My parents divorced when I was a teenager, but they had only recently evolved to a point where they could be in the same room with each other. Obviously, the relationship still had some lingering tension.

"I think he's including all of the Americas," I replied.

"I still think I'm right."

The tour guide stopped and called our group together into a tight huddle. "They use the howl to communicate with each other," he said softly.

"And apparently to have fun watching tourists soil themselves," Pete added.

The tour guide pointed his stick at the howler monkeys overhead. "The howls are actually quite useful as they warn other monkeys of threats."

My mom had been relatively quiet during the tour, so I knew she'd be jumping into the conversation at any time.

"My son makes a similar sound when he tries to sing," my mother told the group. "David, would you like to give the group a brief sample? Just a couple of verses?" This was the obvious payback I had been anticipating for forcing my mom to sing earlier that week, or for the jail story I told the fisherman, or the incident at the restaurant or perhaps for the collective torture to which I continued to subject her. I wasn't sure, and it didn't really matter at that point.

"Absolutely not. I can't really sing."

"It's a perfect time for a quick break," said the tour guide. "Let's hear it."

The rest of the group shouted words of encouragement. I really had no choice. With all attention on me, I closed my eyes, quietly cursed my mother, and began.

"To all the girls I've loved before," I sort of hummed.

"Which is none," Pete shouted.

The others in our group quickly joined in the laughter because it was obvious we were a couple. I rushed through the remainder of the first verse. I could tell from the crowd's reaction that I sucked.

"That was frightening," my mom said. "And you chose a Julio Iglesias song?"

"It's actually a duet," I replied. "With Willie Nelson. You just didn't let me get that far into it."

"Trust me, you went far enough."

Through the group's laughter, the tour guide said, "You're right. He does sound like a howler monkey."

The crowd laughed louder as my face burned with embarrassment. I had a sneaking suspicion that this wouldn't be the last of the ribbing I would experience on this vacation, and boy was I right.

CHAPTER 14

Awergic Weaction

O n the last evening of the vacation we decided to have dinner with a small group of people from the rain forest tour. The group made reservations at the hotel's main restaurant and asked us to join them. We arrived at the restaurant ahead of the other members of the group, so we ordered some appetizers and white wine for the table. After about three sips of the wine, my lips began to tingle. By the time the rest of the group arrived, my lips felt like they were twice their normal size. I was experiencing an allergic reaction to the wine. *Damn Pinot Grigio,* I thought. I could tell the situation was worsening, because the look on each person's face was more horrified than the last.

"What's happening with your lips?" asked one of the tour members. Everyone looked at me.

"Oh, he had some work done earlier," my mom replied. "Botched job."

The guests looked at me more intensely, not sure if they believed my mom's story. My lips were getting bigger by the second, and I knew it would be challenging to speak clearly.

"Dats naught twoo," I muttered. "Ahm habbine an awergic weaction." No one seemed to understand what I was saying. My Pinot Grigio-induced speech impediment fell on deaf ears.

"We tried to tell him not to get Botox injections from a street vendor here in town, but we're only so influential when it comes to his vanity," Pete told the group. "He's got that condition—" he said as he waved his hands wildly, as if that would help him recall the word. "You know the one, that body morph thing."

"Body dysmorphic disorder," my mom said.

"Yes!" Pete cried.

"Weelwee?"

The guests soon caught on that I was experiencing an allergic reaction, and they seemed genuinely concerned. I appreciated the attention, as I would literally need to be asphyxiating and pounding my hands on the table in desperation before getting any reaction from my mom or Pete.

I once had a severe allergic reaction to coconut milk, and Pete had to rush me to the emergency room. When I was stabilized, I texted Pete to let him know he could join me in the recovery room as I was sure he'd be concerned. He returned the text about ten minutes later informing me he was at Home Depot shopping for light bulbs. I recall abruptly ending that text exchange by writing the following:

I hope u purchased painkillers as well. Ur gonna need them.

His response: ☺

My mother wasn't much better. During my childhood she used her own triage technique to determine if her kids' complaints were real emergencies. She would ask the following three questions: Are you missing or unable to move any of your limbs? Is there a fire in the house? Do the police want to speak with me? If we answered no to all three questions, we got a kiss on the forehead and a gentle nudge back outside to play. My chance of getting some sympathy that night was highly unlikely. So instead, I popped an allergy pill and decided to make the most it. Our dinner companions were glad I stuck around, as I was the source of their entertainment for the remainder of the evening.

"Repeat after me, David," said my mother. "Susie collects seashells by the seashore."

"Fwuk wew."

France (2006)

CHAPTER 15

Penis de Milo

A little over a year after our Costa Rica holiday, I decided it was time to venture out again with my mom. I had promised her four trips, and we were at the halfway point. By that time my lips were back to their normal size, and I had successfully forgotten about seeing my mother's baby maker. I left it up to my mom to choose the next destination. She selected Paris. Pete's work schedule often prevents him from taking time off, but he had banked some vacation days, so he decided to join us. None of us had been to Paris before, so we were insanely excited. We planned the trip quickly, and within a few weeks we were on our way.

Pete and I felt it might be wise to go away for a long weekend rather than a full week. Our assumption was that it might be more difficult to get into trouble if we were in Paris for just a few days. We had never been more wrong.

Our first activity was to tour the Louvre. We weren't huge art enthusiasts, but the Louvre was a must-do while visiting Paris. We had just seen Tom Hanks in *The Da Vinci Code* and were intrigued by some of the historical aspects of the museum. We had no idea what we were getting ourselves involved in. After nearly four hours of wandering through the museum's halls, we collapsed onto a small bench right outside the room that housed the Mona Lisa.

"Well, now we know why she's smirking," my mom said.

"Yeah," Pete added. "Who wouldn't smirk at the sight of ten thousand people huddled around you to catch a glimpse? You couldn't even get within twenty feet of it." Not only were people prevented from getting near the exhibit, the painting itself was no larger than a box of Frosted Flakes.

Side note: The museum should distribute bifocals as people enter the exhibit room so that those who aren't farsighted have a fighting chance to actually see the painting.

"Is there a café in this place?" Pete asked. "Can they really expect us to spend all this time here without offering a place to recharge our batteries?"

"There's a food court at the entrance," my mom informed him. "But we're almost done."

"Well, I'm done now," Pete replied. "I can't look at another statue or painting. I'm going to lose my mind." I stood by Pete on this one. I, too, was exhausted and needed to get away from the crowds.

My mom stood up. "Well, there's one last exhibit you'll want to see."

"Oh, yeah? Which one is that?" I asked.

My mother described in great detail the temporary exhibit celebrating the male physique. She told us it was called the Penis de Milo. We, of course, didn't believe a word she told us, but her selling skills were convincing. She went on and on about a conversation she had with the concierge at our hotel, who supposedly told her the exhibit was "scandalous." The clincher for us, however, was the wine tasting she told us would be accompanying the exhibit. I looked at Pete to gauge whether he was in or out.

"If they don't serve wine at this exhibit, we're putting you on a flight back home," Pete told her. She appeared to silently agree. Pete and I decided to give my mother some latitude, so we cautiously followed her down the spacious hall toward the last exhibit. At least another hour passed before I spoke up. My mom rolled her eyes and told us we were nearly at the exhibit. When we finally stumbled into the exhibit room, I was tired and grouchy.

"So much for an exhibition on the male physique," I said. "All I see is this statue with no arms." My mother looked around aimlessly, acting confused and surprised.

"Wait a minute," I said. "This is the *Venus* de Milo. And there aren't any other exhibits in here." My mom pretended she didn't hear me.

"Yeah," Pete added. "And where's the wine?"

"Mom?"

"Well, consider this a gesture of tough love," she replied. "There was no way in hell I was walking all the way back through the museum. This was the only option I had."

"I'm going to give you a five-second head start, and then I'm going to chase you down and tackle you," I told her.

My mom laughed. "For smart men, the two of you fell for that one hook, line, and sinker. I mean, seriously! Penis de Milo?"

In my defense, her selling of the exhibit was skillful. Although Penis de Milo did sound ridiculous, there were other examples of art exhibits that were even more preposterous. I recall my sister and my mom and I gazing at a petrified Neanderthal turd through a sheet of glass at a museum in Portugal. There was a line out the door of people waiting for their turn to stare at it. In comparison, Penis de Milo didn't seem that far-fetched.

My mom continued laughing as we walked out of the exhibit room. "You must be so disappointed."

"I'm actually more upset about the wine," Pete replied. "And just for the record, you're nuts. I just wanted to let you know that."

My mom placed an arm around Pete and kissed him on the cheek. "I love you," she whispered.

"You are *so* buying me a drink later," he said. "And don't you dare tell anyone about this." My mother looked at me and winked.

"It's our little secret," she whispered. Pete still had so much to learn.

CHAPTER 16

Davide Antoinette

The following day we decided to visit the Palace of Versailles. Versailles was located several kilometers outside of Paris, so we rode a train to the historic landmark. The chateaux and the surrounding grounds were breathtaking. While we were touring the outdoor gardens, I felt as though we were in a scene from *Alice in Wonderland*. The colors and shapes of the shrubs and flowers were surreal. Just as we were finishing the garden tour, the skies opened up and surprised us with a heavy rain shower. We ran for cover in the courtyard and decided to join a guided tour inside the palace to escape the inclement weather.

The tour eventually took us to the bedroom of Marie Antoinette, the wife of Louis XVI and the eventual queen of France during the late 1700s. I read that in the tour brochure. I know that because there was no way I would have remembered that fact from fifth grade history class, especially when I can't even name the first three U.S. presidents.

Maria Antoinette's bedroom was quite large, able to accommodate upward of fifty observers. While we were in the room there were four separate tours taking place, each in a different language. The largest group was a Japanese tour. There had to be at least twenty-five people in that group alone. Our tour guide stopped in front of Marie Antoinette's bed and asked us to gather closely. She wore a small microphone that was pinned to her jacket lapel so that members in the back of the group could hear her. As she proceeded to share random facts about certain artifacts and artwork in the room, her focus shifted to a small door to the left of the bed.

"Notice the door," she said as she pointed to it. "This is the closet that Marie Antoinette hid in for three days during the rebellion. Can you imagine what that must have been like for her?" Members of our group ooh'd and ahh'd and jockeyed for position to get the best angle for the perfect picture of a door they'd likely not recall a few years later. Well, that is until my mother decided to speak up.

Side note: Looking back, I remember feeling a sense that something was not quite right. I saw my mom pushing her way through our tour group to get closer to the guide. I should have trusted my instincts and tackled her right then and there.

My mother emerged at the front of the group, leaned into the tour guide's chest so that she could speak directly into the microphone, and proceeded to ruin any chance I had for a normal life. "Hi," she said to the group as she grabbed my arm and pulled me close to her. "I don't mean to cause a distraction, but my son here hid in the closet for twenty years, and there's not a parade of people moving through his bedroom. Am I missing something?" The twenty-five Japanese tourists instantly turned into a mob of paparazzi. There were so many camera flashes going off that I couldn't focus my eyes.

"Wow, that was real," Pete said.

Just when I thought it couldn't get worse, my mother felt the need to elaborate. "Oh, honey, I hope that didn't upset you. I'm sure there was plenty of traffic moving through your bedroom over the years." Two hundred more camera flashes blinded me.

"Are you through now?" I asked her. "I'm adequately humiliated, and I feel like I might need to projectile vomit."

She backed away from the stunned tour guide and gave me a huge hug as if to suggest she was proud of me for all those years I spent in the closet. I wanted to hide under Marie's bed, but after quickly eyeballing the space I determined it would be a tight squeeze. One too many crème brûlées at the Louvre, I suppose. Instead, I reluctantly stuck around for a few group photos and interviews with two Japanese reporters who were on the Versailles tour for a television project.

"You're going to be a huge star in Japan," Pete said.

I raised my eyebrows in mock excitement.

I can see why legit celebrities despise the paparazzi. It took us two hours to escape from the palace. When we finally sat down on the train, I realized that my right palm was chapped from shaking so many hands, and my throat was sore from answering the hundreds of questions thrown at me.

"How many autographs did you sign today?" asked Pete.

"I have no idea."

"They should name the tour after you or give you an honorary nickname," my mom said. "That room probably hasn't seen that much action since Marie Antoinette and what's his lips were living there."

"Louis the Sixteenth," I said.

"How about 'The Closet of Versailles,'" Pete suggested as a possible new name for the tour.

"I got it!" my mom cried. "Davide Antoinette!"

"I love it," Pete said.

And so it stuck. For the remainder of the vacation and for several months afterward, I was affectionately referred to as Davide Antoinette. And people wonder why I have an emotional colon.

United Arab Emirates (2010)

CHAPTER 17

Just the Tip

"This is going to be just like *Sex and the City*," my mom squealed as we settled into our seats for our flight from Washington D.C. to Dubai.

"I hate this game," I replied. "Please tell me you have me earmarked as Mr. Big. I'm not playing the lesbian character again."

"The character isn't lesbian," my mom said. "The actress is."

I rolled my eyes. "Whatever."

Side note: To pass the time, my family occasionally recreated scenes from our favorite television shows and movies. I was never a big fan of our Sex and the City scenes, but you should see our reenactment of the "eat my shit" scene from The Help. *My mother tears up the role of Missus Walters, originally played by Sissy Spacek.*

"You've lost your sense of adventure," my sister Kelly said. "When the hell did that happen?"

"Yeah! Live a little," my mom added.

"Live a little?" I replied. "The fact that you're here with me is ample evidence that I'm willing to take risks."

"I'm not risky," my mother said.

"Are you kidding me? We've pulled you out of a rain gutter in Costa Rica, you tried to eat a tourist in Portugal, and we were basically thrown out of Versailles because you hijacked our tour."

My mother looked at my sister in surprise. "Those are exaggerations. If Pete were here, he would defend me."

I wished Pete were with us. I liked how he played the go-between and distracted my mom so I could focus on things that were important to me, like unnecessary worrying and compulsive thoughts of choking her. Unfortunately, Pete wasn't able to join us on the trip because his military obligations once again kept him stateside. I put my faith in my older sister, Kelly, that she'd be able to keep my mom and me on an even keel during our final trip together. Kelly, like my younger sister Lisa, was practical and levelheaded, although her ability to hold an adult conversation for more than a minute had been severely impacted by the previous ten years she had spent at home raising three children. She often uttered monosyllabic responses to questions, such as yup, nope, duh, and meh, or in some cases she'd jump into a conversation with an ambiguous grunt.

"Mom, just tonight a TSA security dog tackled you because you had a hundred memory cards in your purse," I said.

"I like to take pictures. Is that a crime?"

Kelly let out a deep exhale. "You really are kind of a hot mess, Mom," she said. "But that's why we love you."

"Why does everyone keep telling me that?"

"The only thing I would change about you is that damn lavender sweat suit," I said.

My mom sat up and leaned toward us. "It's my signature outfit. Michael Jackson has his white glove, Judge Judy has her lace collar, and I have my lavender sweat suit. Get over it!"

"Calm down, Samantha," Kelly said. "Here comes the flight attendant. Let's order some drinks."

The flight attendant stopped at our row and engaged the foot brake on the beverage cart. "Hello, something to drink tonight?"

"Yes, we'll take a round of Cosmos," my mom said. The flight attendant laughed. "Take a look around. You're in economy. You can get beer or wine." My mother looked absolutely flabbergasted. "This is economy? Well, someone behind that curtain up there is living my life. I just wanted to let you know that."

"Duly noted," said the smiling attendant.

"Okay, we'll have chardonnay," my mom said as she looked at us for approval. Kelly grunted something that sounded like a yes, and I nodded in agreement. As the flight attendant turned her attention to the drink cart, my mom leaned toward us and said, "This is exactly what's wrong with modern-day aviation."

Our chardonnay and lukewarm curry chicken entrées arrived moments later, and we spent the better part of the following hour dreaming up wild plans for our stay in Dubai. At some point the conversation and chardonnay lulled us to sleep, and before we knew it we were landing.

The flight, although enjoyable, took its toll on us. When we finally arrived at our hotel in downtown Dubai, it was rather late. We grabbed a quick dinner and went straight to our rooms to try to get a good night's sleep. For me, the trip was part work and part play because the headquarters of the business I co-owned with my partner and best friend was located in Dubai. I had committed myself to doing a few administrative tasks while I was in the region. Sleep was an absolute necessity if I was to properly balance business and pleasure.

The next morning, I woke up earlier than I had planned (blame it on jet lag). Rather than lie in bed worrying about things such as whether I had set up my DVR properly so I wouldn't miss *American Idol* or *Toddlers and Tiaras* while I was away, I decided to get dressed and go downstairs to eat breakfast while I waited for my mom and sister to join me. They were notorious for sleeping late, so I knew I had some time to kill.

I approached the host, Enrique, and asked for a table near the window overlooking the courtyard. I knew Enrique because I had stayed at that particular hotel many times on previous trips to the city, and I had become friendly with the staff. Enrique clearly had spent some time at charm school. He had perfect posture, a soft voice, and a tendency to bow his head after every other word. As Enrique escorted me to my table the waiter who had served us the previous night—and who had served me often on my previous stays in that hotel—approached me. It's important to note that most waiters at Dubai hotels are Filipino expats with a heavy accent. The waiter preferred to be called Michael, although I'm sure that was not his real name.

"Mornie, Mr. David," he said.

I smiled politely. "Good morning, Michael."

"You no tip," he told me.

I was still half asleep and a bit grouchy from jet lag, so I wasn't sure if I understood what he was trying to tell me. "Excuse me?"

"You no tip," he said again, now standing right in front of me. He appeared to be upset.

"What do you mean I don't tip?" I said, somewhat irritated. "Are you kidding me?"

Michael looked surprised at my reaction. "Mr. David, you no tip."

This guy has lost his mind, I thought. "This is a free buffet breakfast," I said. "I seat myself, I serve myself, I get my own beverage, and I clean up when I'm done. What is there to tip for?"

Side note: This is when I should have stopped talking.

Michael remained quiet.

"You know, this is the kind of thing that really makes me crazy," I told him. "Everyone has a hand out for money, but no one wants to work. I'm taking a stand here on principle. There are people here who are busting their butts slinging food and drinks all day and night. Those are the ones who should get tips, not the staff members who just watch people eat breakfast."

Michael had a look on his face that suggested he might pass a kidney stone at any moment. "You no tip."

I looked to Enrique for support, but it was pointless because he was shaking uncontrollably and sweating. Apparently they didn't cover the topic of conflict resolution in charm school. I returned my attention to Michael.

"So if you're asking to get a tip for watching me chow down a plate of cold eggs and stale biscuits, you're crazy." I got up and marched toward the table Enrique had pointed out as being mine, but reconsidered. I stopped and turned back to Michael. "And for the record, I'm a huge tipper. For crying out loud, I left you thirty percent last night even though five percent is generous here. I can't even eat now I'm so upset." Enrique took that opportunity to escape and bolted back to the host's station.

Michael looked baffled. "Yes, Mr. David, you left tip at dinner last night and it too much. I can't take." He pulled a few crumpled bills from his pocket and handed them to me.

Side note: Why the hell didn't he just say that first? That would have been the humane thing to do rather than let me carry on like some nut job. And poor Enrique! He's probably still in counseling.

Imagine the surprise on my face. "Oh! That's not the direction I thought this conversation was going in." I placed a hand on his shoulder. "Let's forget everything I just said, shall we? And please, by all means, keep the tip."

Before I had a chance to return the money, Michael said, "You need some tea."

I scanned the room to see how many people had witnessed me hanging myself. Luckily, I didn't see anyone who looked as though they had overhead me. I took a seat at my table and tried to put that conversation behind me. A different waiter hurried over to assist me. Thankfully, I had never met this waiter before.

"Hi, sir," the waiter said. "Coffee, tea, orgy juice?"

"Orgy juice?" I asked, not sure if I had heard him correctly. "That sounds intriguing. How much does that cost?"

"I no understand, sir," replied the waiter.

"No worries. I was just thinking out loud. So is this orgy juice popular?"

The waiter smiled broadly. "Yes, sir. We make fresh every day, and we sell out. I personally squeeze it out every morning." He stretched his arms out wide. "Big batches."

"That's actually disturbing," I said. To this day, I still torture myself by allowing fleeting thoughts run through my mind about what the process of making that orgy juice might look like. "Does your boss know you make this juice?"

The waiter looked surprised at my question. "Yes, sir. He's in the back squeezing out a new batch right now." He pointed to the set of doors behind the breakfast buffet.

I was shocked. "That's even more disturbing," I replied.

The waiter looked more confused. "I no understand, sir."

I needed to solve this mystery. "Can you point to someone who's drinking the orgy juice?"

The waiter looked around briefly and then pointed to a woman sitting at the table behind me. I turned around casually to get a look. "Ahhh, just as I suspected. *That* is orange juice!"

The waiter nodded excitedly in agreement. "Yes, sir, orgy juice."

"I would keep calling it orgy juice. I'm sure it will continue to be a big hit."

The waiter was completely oblivious to my attempt at humor. "So you want?"

"Absolutely. In fact, make it a double."

As the waiter walked away, my mother and sister joined me. The waiter noticed their arrival and turned back and approached our table. "Mornie, ladies," he said. "Coffee, tea, orgy juice?"

Immediately and simultaneously my mother and sister said, "Orgy juice!"

"Don't you even want to know what it is?" I asked them.

My mother placed a hand on my arm and leaned toward me. "I'm sixty-five," she whispered. "I couldn't care less what's in it. It just sounds like it's right in my wheelhouse."

I looked at my sister in shock, hoping for some backup. She remained eerily calm.

"I'm a stay-at-home mother of three," my sister said. "This could be the most fun I've had since those kids were conceived."

The two of them went on for several minutes about things someone like me would or should have no knowledge of such as conception, mammary glands, and female orgasm. As their discussion progressed, I had flashbacks about the five-minute sex education lecture my phys ed coach, Mr. Crandle, facilitated in front of my homeroom class in junior high school. He awkwardly walked over to the television cart, picked up the loose cord, pointed to the prongs on the plug, and shoved it into the electrical socket on the wall. "That," he said, "is basically how sexual intercourse works."

I was terrified for years afterward thinking that to come of age, I'd have to stick my penis into a live electrical outlet. And when I heard about guys needing to wear a "rubber" during sex, the fear of possibly dying from electrical shock was firmly cemented into my brain well into my late teens. I'm such an idiot.

"I'm sorry to interrupt your vagina monologues," I said, "but I'm a bit disappointed."

"Oh, boy, here we go," my mother said.

"You're supposed to be role models for me, and on your first day in Dubai you're ordering orgy juice? Seriously?" I looked down and shook my head dramatically. As I raised my head the waiter returned to our table.

"Here's your double orgy juice, sir," he said as he placed the enormous glass in front of me.

My mother grinned. "Drink your juice, Shelby."

CHAPTER 18

Prison Bitch

After breakfast, my sister returned to her room to prepare herself for a morning of shopping while my mom and I made a quick stop at the hotel gift shop.

"Oh, look!" my mom shouted from across the shop. "They have refrigerator magnets of the Burj Khalifa!" She held one up for me to see. "Look how cute they are."

I contemplated ignoring her, but we made eye contact, so I felt compelled to respond. "You can't possibly have any free space on your fridge."

"Maybe they're gifts," she said as she dumped a handful of fridge magnets into her shopping basket and headed toward the tacky knickknack section. I approached the clerk with a granola bar that didn't have a price on it. I wanted to get some relatively healthy snacks for my room so that I wouldn't be tempted to eat the crap in the minibar.

"How much are the granola bars?

The clerk didn't look up from the book he was reading. "Four dirhams or two for ten."

"That doesn't make sense. You mean each one is more expensive if you buy two?" The clerk looked up at me. I could see him trying to process what I had said. "Is this a way for the government to prevent overeating?" I added, trying to engage in some lighthearted fun. He wasn't biting.

"It's a special we have this month."

"Just out of curiosity, how much if I buy three?"

"Twelve dirhams."

I scratched my head. "I'm totally confused. Now we're back to the original unit price?" I didn't think it possible, but the clerk looked even more disinterested.

"It's a special."

"Never mind. I'll just take one." I placed the granola bar on the counter.

"Five dirhams, please."

"What? I thought you said they were four dirhams each."

The clerk looked annoyed. "Only if you buy two. If not, they're five dirhams each."

I had a feeling he was intentionally toying with me. I had seen him talking to the waiter, Michael, a few minutes earlier, so I assumed this exchange was my punishment.

"Okay, I get it," I said, nearing exhaustion. "How much are the sparkling waters?"

"Twelve dirhams. But if you get a granola bar, too, it's twenty dirhams."

"Please stop," I begged.

Side note: You may be wondering why I included a story about granola bars, but this story really has more to do with my mother's obsession with refrigerator magnets.

My mother walked up next to me and placed her items on the counter. "Oh, granola bars!" she said. "My doctor tells me I'm supposed to eat more fiber."

"Maybe you should consider adding Metamucil to your chardonnay," I said. I paused for a moment to admire how quickly I came up with that reply, and then I elaborated. "But then again you might overdose on the Metamucil."

My mom pursed her lips in disapproval. "You're on a roll today."

"How much?" she asked the clerk as she held up the granola bar.

The clerk looked directly at me when he replied, "Four dirhams, ma'am."

If my mother's basket of fridge magnets and miniature desert snow globes had not been blocking my access to the counter, I would have seriously considered lunging over it. I suppose I should be somewhat grateful she's obsessed with refrigerator magnets or I could still be serving time in a Dubai prison. I think it's safe to say that I would not have fared well in a Middle East prison. At that time I weighed about one fifty (soaking wet) and had a baby face with "open for business" written all over it. In fact, that exchange in the gift shop is what motivated me to learn enough Arabic to confidently say, *Hello, big guy. I'd like to be your bitch during my stay here in exchange for protection. What do you say?* One can never be overly prepared.

CHAPTER 19

Run, Forrest, Run!

Later that day, the three of us set out into the desert for a safari thrill tour. The tour was comprised of a rather harrowing drive in an SUV through the rolling dunes near the Oman border, a camel ride, and an evening at a desert fortress, where you were expected to eat food you didn't recognize and sit idly in the stifling humidity while you swatted flies away from your face and sweated out every last drop of moisture in your body.

Regardless, the ride through the dunes was actually quite enjoyable. It reminded me of a shaky rollercoaster, except for the occasional stops we had to make to allow caravans of camels to cross our path. I found it intriguing that the camels, although essentially wild, had rope connecting their front and back legs. The rope had just enough slack to allow the camels to walk.

"Why do those camels have rope attached to their legs?" I asked our driver.

He looked at the camels to our left. "So the park rangers can catch them if needed," he replied.

"I'm not sure I follow."

"Camels can run very fast," he informed us. "The rope prevents them from running away."

My mom leaned forward. "Camels can run? I always thought they were slow."

"Me, too," I added. "Now I want to see one run."

The driver laughed. "Camels don't run often, but when they do, it's a thing of beauty."

As we drove out of the dunes toward the desert fortress, I looked back several times to catch a glimpse of the camels, which were now nothing more than silhouettes against the red hue of the setting sun. They were so beautiful and, for me, they symbolized life on the Arabian Peninsula. Well, that was until I actually hopped onto one and took it for a ride, but I'll get to that in just a moment. When we pulled up to the front of the gated fortress, I knew the evening's experience was about to take a steep dive south.

"You call this a fortress?" I asked.

"Yes, sir," said the driver.

"Who lived here? Hobbits?"

We exited the SUV and looked around. The fortress was essentially a short wooden stockade fence that formed a border around a large rectangular area of the desert.

"Y'all might want to hop onto Wikipedia later and look up the word *fortress*," I said. "You know, just to get a comparison or maybe to spark a few ideas about how to spruce the place up a bit."

The driver looked as though he couldn't have cared less about what I was saying. He pointed to a row of camels near the left side of the entrance to the fortress. "Camel ride?"

I looked at my mom and sister. They seemed to like the idea. "Sure," I replied.

We walked over to the young man who apparently was responsible for coordinating the camel rides. He held one of the camels by a leash as he reached out to shake my hand. "You go for a ride?"

"Yes, please," I replied.

He pointed to my mom and motioned for her to approach him. "I'll help you up first." He jerked the leash, and the camel slowly dropped to its knees. "First time on a camel?" he asked my mom.

She nervously approached the camel. "Yes."

"It'll be good. Isn't that right, Chardonnay?" he said as he patted the camel's head.

My mom turned to my sister and me and smiled. "My camel's name is Chardonnay!"

I leaned toward my sister. "She must be in heaven right now."

My mother clumsily climbed atop the camel's back and motioned to the young man that she was in position. The man tugged the leash again, and the camel jerked its body forward and stood up. My sister and I proceeded to climb onto our respective camel. Once we were all on board, the young man led the camels into an open area across from the wooden structure the tour guide insisted on referring to as the fortress.

"Wow, these camels are tall," Kelly said.

"I know," I replied. "It's like a whole different atmosphere up here."

My sister yelled to the young man, "What's my camel's name?"

"Champagne."

"And mine?" I asked.

The young man turned and looked up at me. "Forrest Hump."

"My camel's name is Forrest Hump?"

"Yes, he's quite fast, and there's no rope around his legs. Just make sure you don't smack him on the backside," he said as he winked.

"That might be tough for him," my mom told the young man.

"Funny, Mom," I said. I was lagging behind the other two camels, so I tried to encourage Forrest Hump to catch up.

"Come on, boy," I said. "Get up there."

My sister turned around to see where I was. "What are you doing back there?"

"Trying to catch up. I thought my camel was fast." Just as I made that statement, something stung the back of my neck. A horsefly. I attempted to swat it away, but it decided to fight back. "Is anyone else getting eaten alive by horseflies?" No response. I felt the pinch of another bite. This time the bite occurred on my left calf. I spotted the culprit and followed the fly in flight until it landed behind the camel's saddle. I focused on it, held my hand up, and swatted it. "Got it," I whispered. I then realized that I had just smacked the camel on its backside. *Oh, crap*, I thought.

Side note: When the young man warned me that the camel was fast, I imagined a nice, steady gallop. I did not expect Forrest Hump to take off like fucking Seabiscuit.

"Help!" I screamed as Forrest and I flew past Chardonnay and Champagne.

"Where are you going?" my mom yelled.

"I'm guessing an early grave," I yelled back. By the time I finished screaming I had already left the others in the dust. I tried to reason with Forrest Hump to get him to slow down. "There, there, Forrest," I said softly while I rubbed the side of his head as if I had suddenly become the camel whisperer. Forrest Hump wasn't having any of it. He continued to run and buck as though he were auditioning for the final spot in a rodeo. When I let go of his leash to try to comfort him, the situation took a disastrous turn. With only one hand to hold myself steady, I lost my balance and slipped off Forrest Hump's back.

This cannot be happening, I thought as I assessed the situation. I was in the precarious position of having my right leg still hooked over Forrest Hump's back and my left leg dragging in the sand. You'd think he would have slowed down. Nope. As we made our second pass in front of my mom and sister, who by the way had stopped to enjoy watching the scene unfold, I tried to free myself. That didn't work out so well. My right foot got caught in the leash as I fell to the ground and skidded across the red sand.

Side note: None of this was mentioned in the marketing brochure the concierge gave us.

"David, are you okay?" my mom asked as Forrest Hump bolted past her with me in tow.

"Uh-huh," I yelled back, but not with much confidence.

When Forrest Hump finally came to a stop, I laid motionless on the ground. My mother and sister rushed over to me.

"Do you think he's okay?" asked Kelly.

My mom patted Forrest Hump's side. "I think he'll be fine. He probably just got startled."

"I meant David."

My mom looked down at me. "Oh, yes, of course. Honey, are you okay?"

I was lying on my back with my eyes closed. "Me? Am *I* okay? Why wouldn't I be okay?"

"It looked like you had a rough ride there," my mom replied while holding back a modest laugh.

"I was nearly dragged to death by a psychotic camel, and I'm fairly sure I've lost the top layer of skin on my exposed body parts. But don't worry about me. I'm fine. Really."

"Oh, you poor thing," my mother said but without the degree of sympathy I was hoping for.

"And I may never get the skin back on my left ass cheek," I added.

"I thought you said you lost skin only on your exposed body parts?" Kelly said.

I rolled over slightly. "Ohhhhh!" cried my mom and sister as they looked down at my bare ass.

"Look at the bright side," my mom said as she untangled my foot from the leash. "We still have several days left of our vacation, and I'm willing to bet that tonight's ride will be just a faint memory by the time we leave."

I was leaning toward not believing her, but given the past three vacations, anything was possible. "You guys can go ahead to dinner. I'll meet you in a few minutes. I want to retrace the camel's steps to see if I can find my self-confidence."

Mom grabbed my arm to help me up. "Oh, honey," she said. "I don't think you'll find it in the sand. Don't you think you lost your self-confidence on that hill in Lisbon a few years back?"

I stood up and brushed the sand off my face and chest. "Don't take this the wrong way," I replied, "but I hope you choke on a kafta ball tonight at dinner."

"There's the David we love," she replied. She kissed me on the forehead.

I decided to abandon the search for my self-confidence and instead joined my mom and sister as they walked into the fortress.

"You really got some air on that joy ride," Kelly said. "Were you scared?"

"I'm not ready to talk about it just yet. Once I get my spine back in order and I've dug all of the sand out of my ass crack, I'll be in a better position to take questions."

"I see a gift shop!" my mom squealed. "Kelly, let's go check it out." She turned to me. "We'll be back in a bit."

I kept walking toward the sitting area. "I'll be over by the lanterns counting my teeth," I told them. I was too late. My mom and Kelly had already disappeared behind a row of handmade scarves. *If my mother brings me back a refrigerator magnet with a picture of Forrest Hump on it,* I thought, *I'm going to spend the remainder of the evening in the men's room slamming a plunger against my face.*

About an hour later, Kelly and my mom plopped themselves down at our dinner table. They both were sporting a henna tattoo. Kelly had elected to have her hands done while my mom chose to have her tattoo inked just below her left collarbone.

"Isn't it beautiful?" my mom said as she pulled her shirt down so I could see the entire tattoo. "It's an Arabic phrase."

"David, you can read some Arabic. Do you know what it says?" Kelly asked.

I leaned in and squinted at my mom's tattoo. "All-you-can-eat buffet for ten ninety-nine."

My mom sighed. "You are such a smartass." I shrugged. "Oh, that reminds me," she continued. "I bought you something from the gift store." She handed me a small paper bag.

My small intestine immediately seized up, and I began to sweat. I had forgotten that my mother always gets even. I don't know how that slipped my mind.

"I know how fond you are of refrigerator magnets."

CHAPTER 20

Screaming Children

The following morning I got up early, mostly because of repeated nightmares of a toilet plunger striking my face, so I decided to tackle some work I needed to get done before the end of the day. My lower back felt as though an elephant had performed a pirouette on it, and I still couldn't put pressure on my left ass cheek. I had to sit on my doughnut-shaped airplane pillow to ease the pain. After about an hour of working, someone knocked on my door. My mom and sister were at the spa, so I didn't know who it could be. The last thing I needed was an interruption.

When I opened the door, I was face to face with a female employee of the hotel. Well, that's not entirely true. I was indeed greeted by a female employee of the hotel, but we were not at the same eye level. I stood at about six feet, and she couldn't have been taller than the height of the doorknob.

"It's a good thing I didn't use the peephole," I said. "I would have missed you."

The woman didn't look impressed with the joke. "Hi, sir," she said. "I'm doing a quality check to make sure your stay is going well." I stood with a rather wide stance, so the woman used the opportunity to peer between my legs to survey the condition of my room.

"Okay."

"Is there anything we can do to improve your experience with us?" she asked as she returned her attention to me.

I wasn't sure if I should simply give her the obligatory response such as extra bottles of water in the room or an additional blanket or if I should go big. I opted to go big.

"Yes," I replied. "Now that I think about it, it would be great if there were fewer children running around and fewer interruptions from staff."

"Less children?"

"That's right. I'm not sure what's going on at the hotel this week, but it appears there are an inordinate number of kids here."

"Ah, yes," she replied. "We're hosting an event."

I raised my eyebrows in mock surprise. "Oh? Let me guess. A program for children with severe attention deficit disorder?"

The woman's facial expression made it clear I was wrong.

"Bipolar kiddie camp?"

The woman frowned. "No, it's a youth leadership program sponsored by our hotel. It's designed to teach kids skills such as respect and appreciation of other cultures."

"Well, that all sounds great, but I do have a suggestion." She waited silently for me to continue. "I would either add 'tiptoeing down hallways' to the course objectives or I'd fire the program facilitator."

"I'm the program facilitator."

The conversation had officially become awkward. I'm actually a patient person, but that particular morning I was irritable. Perhaps the aches and pains from the previous night's near-death camel pull had gotten the best of me. The woman was nice enough, and she seemed passionate about her leadership program. I owed it to her to stay engaged. "Let's not throw the towel in just yet," I said. "With a bit of polishing and refinement, I'm sure you'll catch on and be quite successful." As soon as I uttered those words, I knew I had blown it.

The woman lowered her notebook and placed her free hand on her hip. "I've been running the program for four years. We've graduated over two hundred children."

To be honest, two hundred seemed kind of low to me for a four-year stretch, but I was by no means an expert on the rehabilitation of young minds or whatever it was she was doing with those kids. I felt an urgent need to end this conversation quickly.

"I'm closing the door in thirty seconds before I say anything else incriminating."

"Thank you for your time sir," she said, still frowning at me.

I thanked her as well and closed the door. After about two minutes, there was another knock on the door. The same woman greeted me.

"Hi, sir. I just wanted to double-check that less children and less interruptions were the only two items you feel we needed to address." She hung on the word *interruptions* just long enough to sound antagonistic.

"Yes, that's it," I said. She stood there quietly, staring up at me. I lifted an eyebrow, silently asking her if there was anything else she needed.

"Okay, thank you, sir. Have a nice day."

I closed the door. About five minutes later, the phone rang. It was the same woman.

"Hi, sir. I'm sorry to bother you again, but I forgot to ask if you had any laundry today or if you needed any service items like shampoo or more towels."

I really ticked her off, I thought. "No, thank you, I'm all set." She thanked me again, and we ended the call. I took a deep breath and sat down on the edge of the bed. A moment later came another knock on the door. I walked over to the door and opened it. A young man in a housekeeping uniform greeted me.

"Hi, sir," he said. "I'm doing a quality check to see if there's anything we can do to improve your stay."

I rubbed my closed eyes with my fingers and took a deep breath. "Am I in the twilight zone?" The man looked confused. "I'm serious," I continued. "Or did my mom put you up to this?"

"Sorry?"

"Never mind. I already submitted feedback. Fewer interruptions and fewer children." The man wrote something on his notepad. "That's not a problem, sir. Thank you for your time." I closed the door and returned to the bed. Less than a minute later there was another knock on the door. It was the same man.

"Hi, sir. I forgot to ask if you had any laundry or if you needed any service items."

Side note: I wanted to drop the F-bomb so badly, but I knew that wouldn't go over well seeing as how I was in an Islamic country.

"Can I borrow your pen?" I asked. "I'm thinking about jabbing it into my eye sockets."

"That's funny," he said.

"I'm actually serious." The man's smile gave way to an expression of panic. "I'm all set on laundry, but thank you for asking." I closed the door and turned on the television. Five minutes later, the phone rang.

"Hi, Mr. David," said a woman whose voice I didn't recognize. "I'm calling from the front desk to apologize as I understand our quality check came to you twice today."

"That's okay." I told her.

"Brilliant," she said. "While I have you on the phone, Mr. David, are you in need of any service items?"

I couldn't believe what I was hearing. A searing pain shot through my lower abdomen. *These people are on a mission to prevent me from having a healthy digestive system*, I thought. *I just know it.*

"Is business slow today?" I asked.

"Sorry, sir?"

"Am I the only guest in the hotel? I've spent the last thirty minutes answering the same questions. I know you must think that I'm on holiday and I'm holed up in my room watching television and eating overpriced granola bars, but I happen to be working." There was silence on the other end. "Notice on my room order that I have the business package with high-speed Internet and a desk. Did you think I ordered that just for shits and giggles? Well, the answer is no. I ordered those things because I'm a businessman. Businessmen need long periods of time to concentrate on work. Can you hear my strained voice? I'm actually getting a sore throat from talking so much today to hotel staff." The women remained silent. "And just in case you're curious, every time I'm interrupted a small piece of my sanity disappears. Poof. Gone. By the time I'm required to check out, I'll be huddled in a corner of my room talking to myself and picking at my own skin. Visualize that for a moment. Is that what you're hoping for?"

"Of course not, sir."

"Well, I would hope not. It doesn't seem like a very good business model to kill off all of your priority guests."

"So you are all set on towels and water, Mr. David?" she asked.

"More than I can tell you." I hung up the phone and sat on the edge of the bed, exhausted. That's when I heard it. Screaming children in the hall.

CHAPTER 21

Give Me an I. Give Me a B. Give Me an S.

J ust before lunch my mom dropped by my room and asked if I would be willing to join her on a brief shopping trip to one of the flagship malls in the city. She informed me that Kelly was still at the spa and wouldn't be free until the evening. I had little desire to go shopping, but I needed to make a quick visit to our corporate bank, which had a large branch near the Mall of the Emirates.

"I'll go shopping with you if you join me on a trip to the bank," I said.

"That's doesn't sound so bad."

I chuckled. "Trust me. Every time I go to this bank I have a nervous breakdown."

My mom looked confident. "I think the two of us can handle it."

Side note: The banks in the UAE are often viewed as places where locals amuse themselves by testing the mental aptitude and endurance of unwitting westerners.

I gave my mother another opportunity to back out, but she had made up her mind. She was coming along for the experience. I gathered some paperwork, and within a few minutes we were in a taxi. When we arrived at the bank, we hurried toward to the business support center. We took a number from the customer service ticket machine and sat down on one of the half dozen bright pink couches in the lobby.

"They just called number one seventy-eight," my mom said. "What number do we have?"

"Six nineteen."

My mom looked around the lobby. "But there's no one else here."

"I know. I told you this place was bizarre. We just need to hold it together and patiently power through this process."

"One seventy-nine," said a man over the intercom. "Now serving one seventy-nine at kiosk three." My mom and I looked around. The room was still empty. I looked over to the row of service kiosks. There were five kiosks open, and the young lady at the third kiosk sat silently as she stared out at the empty lobby from behind her hijab.

"One-eighty," said the same man over the intercom, and again nobody moved. After nearly an hour of listening to an anonymous man with a calming British accent call out numbers, we finally heard ours. We jumped up and ran to kiosk four.

"Hi, how are you today?" I asked the woman behind the desk.

"I'm fine. Welcome to our bank," she replied. "Please have a seat."

My mom and I took a seat on the opposite side of the desk from where the woman was seated. Before I was able to describe to the woman the reason why we were there, she entered into a brief monologue about the monthly promotions the bank was offering. I leveraged the opportunity to assess the woman to gauge how much trouble might come our way. I didn't see any sign of good news. She looked tough. I couldn't determine her age from first glance, but she had to be well above sixty. Her voice reinforced my observation. She sounded gritty, as if she had spent a significant portion of her adult life puffing on the end of a shisha pipe. She wore a teal headscarf and a light gray pantsuit, but neither did anything to soften her appearance.

"My goal is to exceed your expectations today. How may I help you?"

I already didn't believe a word she said. "I need to transfer funds from one of my accounts to another. It's quite urgent."

"Did you try logging in to your account on our website?"

I took a deep breath. "Yes, of course, but it's not working. That's why I'm here."

"Oh, my," she said. "Are you here on your lunch break?"

I lowered my head. "I'm already getting anxious. Is this going to take long?"

The woman opened a drawer in a file cabinet located below her desk and pulled out a stack of paper. "I just need you to fill out this form, and then we'll have a look at it."

I took the form and thumbed through it. "It's fourteen pages!"

"I would suggest you press hard."

My mother leaned toward me and whispered, "She's a lovely woman."

I didn't have to ask if she was joking, because I could feel the sarcasm.

I labored over the form for what seemed like several hours. "Here you go," I said as I handed the reams of paper back to the representative. She snatched the stack of paper from my hand and immediately flipped to the last page to confirm that I had signed it.

"Okay, let me take this to verify your signature, and then we'll take it from there. I'll be back in a few minutes."

Twenty-four minutes and nineteen seconds went by before she returned. "I thought you got lost," I said. The woman had a smile on her face, which for a moment helped to relax me, but that turned out to be short-lived.

"I have bad news," she informed me. "Your signature failed authentication."

"How is that possible? It's my signature." The woman sat down behind her desk. "The signature on the form does not match the one we have on record."

"What exactly is the issue?" my mom asked.

The woman picked up her reading glasses and put them on. "The T on today's signature is crossed differently than the T on the original signature specimen we have."

I shifted uncomfortably in my seat. "Are you for real?"

"Yes, sir. We cannot accept this signature." Not only did the woman's answer infuriate me, but so, too, did the casual way in which she delivered the information. "Ma'am, with all due respect, I signed that specimen over three years ago when I opened the account here."

The woman shifted papers on her desk as if preparing for the conversation to end.

"Signatures are a reflection of a person's life experience," I said. "A lot has happened in those three years. No one signs the same way twice."

The woman stopped shuffling papers and looked at me. "I'm sorry."

"This is ridiculous," my mom said. "Can't he give a blood sample or pee in a cup?"

The woman did not look amused. "We rely solely on signature specimens."

"This seems like a sophisticated bank," my mom said. "You'd think you would have one of those retina scanners or something he can press his fingers against to have his prints read."

"I have my passport with me," I said. I handed it to her. "Check out my signature."

The woman flipped through the passport. "Your signature on the passport is also different, sir."

I sighed heavily and began to tap my foot. "Listen, I opened the stupid account. I own the business. And now I can't even transfer funds because my signatures don't match exactly. This is unacceptable." I could feel the early signs of an IBS attack coming on. My mother must have heard the rumbling, because she immediately jumped back into the discussion.

"There has to be something you can do to help him," my mom said. As my mom completed her appeal, I slipped out of my chair from exhaustion. "Look," my mom said. "He's even got one knee on the ground. Can't you see he's begging?"

"I'd raise my hand in a salute as well, but it's cramped from pressing so hard on that form," I added.

"Let me see what I can do," said the woman. "I'll be right back."

I sat back up in my seat.

"Please don't be gone for a half hour again," I pleaded. "I feel weak. I could literally expire at any moment."

"I'll send someone by with tea," she said.

"And biscuits, please," I begged.

Twenty-six minutes and fifty seconds ticked by (and no tea service, by the way) before the woman returned.

"No luck," she said. "You will need to get your new signature approved at the U.S. embassy here in Dubai and then return."

"You're joking, right?" I asked. "Why would I need to get

my signature approved by the U.S. embassy? I came here today requesting a simple transaction. You have overcomplicated this to the point of literally forcing me into a near panic attack." I stood up. "Didn't you say in your introduction that your goal was to exceed my expectations? You're not doing that very well."

My mom glared at the woman with a look that one would expect just before being sucker punched. I think the woman picked up on my mother's growing frustration.

"Give me a few more moments to see if I can get some movement on this from a different manager," the woman said.

When she stood up and started to walk away, I gently grabbed her arm. "Before you go, I want to give you a visual. If I leave here today and my funds are not transferred, I am going to lose my mind. Do you understand that? I will lose it." No reaction came from the woman. "Did you ever see *The Exorcist*? Remember the spinning head and the green vomit and the bad words? Well, that will be me. I'll sit right here, in this very seat, and soil myself while I drop F-bombs."

The woman tugged herself free of my grip and turned away. This time my mom grabbed the woman's arm.

"Trust me, I nearly had to perform an exorcism on him when he was a child," she said. "If he's forced into that dark place again, I'm the one who will be required to escort him back to the U.S. And I'm not a young woman. The trip could push me to the brink as well. Is that what you want?" The woman shook her head. "Well, as you leave us to go into that back office for God only knows how long, we wanted to leave you with those thoughts."

When I caught a glimpse of the woman walking toward us, I looked up at the clock on the wall behind her desk and estimated that she'd been gone for a solid forty-five minutes. "Sorry for the delay," she said.

"That's okay," I said. "I used the time to practice my head spins."

The woman plopped herself down into her seat. "I have good news. We approved your funds transfer as a one-time exception."

"Yes! Yes!" I screamed as I jumped out of my seat and gave my mom a high-five. I can recall only a handful of times when I've felt more exhilarated, most notably the time when I scored the sea bass in my victory over that old Portuguese woman at the espresso shop in Lisbon. I looked down the row of teller kiosks to witness other exhausted customers staring at me with palpable jealously. I felt guilty for my visible display of exuberance.

"In the future, you can always perform this transaction online," the woman said. "It takes about three minutes, and it's free."

My mother stood up and lifted her purse from the floor and slung it over her shoulder. "We're going to forget those words came out of your mouth, as a one-time exception," she said.

The woman had clearly moved on because she sat quietly at her desk shuffling papers in yet another attempt to usher us to the end of the discussion. "Is there anything else I can help you with?" asked the woman.

Reluctantly, I took the bait. "Actually, yes. I need to open a line of credit."

Side note: What the hell was I thinking? My decision to not run screaming from the bank at that very moment will likely haunt me for the remainder of my life.

"I'll walk you over to your client engagement specialist, who can help you with that process. But, before I do," she said, "I'm obligated to ask whether I succeeded today in exceeding your expectations."

"Remember the head spins I talked about earlier? I feel one coming on. So I would suggest you just take me to my client engagement specialist."

The woman, who by this point was more than happy to dump

us off onto someone else, quickly led us to the other side of the business center, where she handed us off to a stocky Indian man named Sandeep.

"Hi, Mr. Robert. How are you?" he asked. He shook my hand and then my mom's.

"I just came from the business support center," I said. "What do you think?"

"Ah, yes. That can be interesting," he said. "Can I get you some tea?"

We sat down on one of the white leather couches that were huddled in the middle of that area of the bank. "Yes, that would be great," I replied. My mom declined the offer.

"How do you take it?" Sandeep asked me.

I set my briefcase on the floor in front of me. "Normally I take it black, but after today's experience my electrolytes are all thrown off, so I'll take it with sugar and milk."

Sandeep waved over a young man and gave my order to him. The young man nodded and walked away.

"You might want to think about installing an oxygen machine in the lobby so clients can take a hit or two from it to generate enough energy to fight their way through all the red tape here."

Sandeep yawned. "I'll take that into consideration. While we wait for tea, tell me about your current situation."

For the next several minutes I opened up about how the previous exchange that morning had flared up my IBS and how my mother thought I was running a mild fever. I assured Sandeep that I wasn't going to pursue a formal complaint, although both my mom and I were concerned that the color hadn't returned to my face, which could be a sign of shock.

The young man returned and handed me my tea. I took a huge gulp. "Even when I was a child," I said, talking much faster, "the smallest little thing would put me into an emotional tailspin. I like having a routine. Chaos makes me crazy." I turned back to my mother. "Are you sure my color isn't back yet?"

Sandeep cleared his throat and sat up. "I was thinking more along the lines of your current business situation."

I wanted to die right there on the couch. I had just spent the previous few minutes sharing my medical history with a complete stranger who I thought actually cared about me.

"That's embarrassing," my mom whispered to me.

"I'm here to open a line of credit," I said. I wasn't even sure if I was talking out loud, because my cheeks were numb from embarrassment.

"How much are you looking to leverage?" Sandeep asked.

I shared with Sandeep how much my business was looking to borrow.

"That shouldn't be a problem. In order to move forward we will just need to put a freeze on that same amount in your account until the line of credit is closed."

I placed my cup of tea on the coffee table in front of me. "I'm sorry, did I hear that correctly? Why would you freeze funds in my account?"

"We don't use that money," he replied. "We just hold it for collateral."

One thing I love about my mother is that she can remain quiet when required, but when you needed her to spring into action, she was always ready to go. She said, "Why the hell would he ask for the money if he already had it in his account?"

Sandeep shifted uncomfortably. "I can see you're both getting upset."

I stood up. "Upset? I'm not upset. I'm actually quite calm. I'm just trying to get my head around this giant load of nonsense you just dropped into my lap. Banks lend money. Isn't that what they do?"

Sandeep also stood up. "Yes, but after the financial crisis in 2009 we changed our policy."

"Oh, blame it on a policy. I see. Okay, you know what, I'm gonna create a policy right now." I started to draw a circle around myself by dragging my foot across the carpet. "I don't want any stupidity within a fifteen-foot radius of me." Sandeep looked on in disbelief as I continued drawing my imaginary circle. "Mom, pick your feet up," I said as I tried to close the circle in front of where she sat.

"Are you sure you're okay, sir? You're acting a bit crazy."

"I'm not crazy!" I shouted. "See that lady over there?" I pointed to the woman my mom and I had just dealt with. "*She's* crazy! That's what crazy looks like."

The man didn't look at the woman I pointed to and instead stared directly at me. "You just drew a stupidity circle on the carpet with your foot."

My mother stood up. "We've been here since eleven-thirty this morning." It's five o'clock in the afternoon now. We haven't seen the sun all day. If we stay here any longer we're going to need a vitamin D supplement."

Sandeep stepped toward me. "I wish I could help."

"You're in the circle," I told him. "Remember the rules?"

He looked down and stepped back.

"This is ridiculous," my mom yelled. "Let's get out of here." She grabbed my arm and led me toward the glass revolving door. We exited the bank and had every intention of never coming back until I realized I had left my briefcase on the floor next to the couch. I walked back into the bank and approached the side of the couch where I left my briefcase. Sandeep was still seated in the same position, probably trying to erase us from his memory.

"I forgot my briefcase," I said as I leaned down and picked it up. "But now I'm really leaving this evil bank. You should be ashamed of yourself." And with that I stormed off toward the door.

Side note: Let this be a lesson to never attempt a dramatic exit unless you've fully scoped out your strategy, including plans B and C.

As I stepped into the revolving door I heard a loud pop followed by a high-pitched whining and then several seconds of silence. The power supply had crapped the bed. I pushed on the door. Nothing. I turned and pushed it backward. Nothing. I was stuck. I looked for my mom, but she was nowhere in sight. *Damn! She abandoned me,* I thought. I turned around and peered into the bank lobby. Sandeep was still sitting on the couch. I pressed my nose against the glass and knocked.

Sandeep looked up.

"Hi," I said in a gentle, childlike voice. "Remember me? The crazy one?"

Sandeep looked at me with indifference.

"I know this probably brings you a tremendous amount of pleasure, but I think I'm stuck. Can you help me out?"

Sandeep didn't budge.

"We can forget about the circle. Let's just chalk that up to my dehydration and stress. Okay?" *Can he even hear me?* I thought. "I'm feeling better now," I said louder. "Look!" I jumped up and down a few times and flapped my arms. "I just want to go home now. Can you let me out? Please?"

Sandeep shook his head.

Oh, my God, I thought. *He isn't going to help me.* "Technically, I think you're required to help me. Didn't you take an oath or something? Sandeep seemed to enjoy my predicament. He slowly lifted his cup of tea and took a few measured sips. After his last sip, he had a subtle smile on his face. His wasn't a normal smile. It was the type of smile that appears on a person's face when they've cornered an opponent and can clearly see victory within reach. I've seen that smile on my mother's face far too many times.

"It's getting hot in here," I cried. "I'm not going to last very long in this tiny space." I realized how stupid my plea was because I'm sure Sandeep was sticking around only to watch me emotionally disintegrate. I caught a movement out of the corner of my eye and realized it was my lavender superhero standing on the other side of the glass door.

"Stand back," my mom yelled as she got into position. "I'm going to bust you out of there, sweetheart." As my mom swung her purse over her head, I recalled that several years earlier she had taken a similar stance in front of a ticket kiosk in Boston. I knew what was coming, so I braced myself for impact. With just one strike, I was a free man. I never looked back to see Sandeep's reaction. I didn't have the time. The jolt to the revolving door set off the bank's alarm system, and my mom and I thought it best that we disappear quickly.

"That was intense," my mom said as we hustled to the main road to wave down a taxi. As a taxi pulled over, I hugged my mom and thanked her for rescuing me.

We dived into the taxi. "Well, I couldn't just leave you there. Besides, I wouldn't know how to get back to the hotel."

I deserved that jab because if it weren't for me, she wouldn't have had to endure that exhausting experience at the bank, even though I had warned her several times.

"Mall of the Emirates, please," I told the driver. "I think we make a good superhero team," I said to my mom. She nodded. "But I need a special weapon." I glanced at my mom's oversized quilted purse. "We know what yours is. But what's mine?"

My mother placed her hand on my leg yet turned away from me and stared out the window. "The ability to wear people down with obsessive compulsiveness and incessant worrying."

I suppose I deserved that jab, too. "So anxiety is my secret weapon?" I asked, slightly disappointed.

"Do you think Wonder Woman was completely thrilled with

her wristbands and lasso? We all have to play with the cards we were dealt."

"Well, it's a twenty-minute drive to the mall," I said. "I think I'll use this time to refine my secret weapon."

My mother pulled her purse up onto the seat between us and patted it several times.

"You go right ahead, sweetheart. You go right ahead."

CHAPTER 22

There's No L in Chardonnay

During the rescue mission to free me from the revolving door, my mom and I had worked up a healthy appetite. We also agreed we needed a stiff drink after the crazy day we had endured. This left us with only a few options at the mall, because most restaurants were not permitted to serve alcoholic beverages unless they were located within a western hotel. Luckily, there was a large hotel inside the mall with a restaurant I frequented often when I was in town.

The host walked us to our table at the front of the restaurant near the expansive windows that overlooked the mall's indoor ski resort and handed us menus. Our waiter came over immediately to greet us.

"Welcome and good afternoon!" he said with a rather thick Persian accent. "Where are you from?"

"The States," I replied.

The waiter's eyes lit up. "Which state is that?"

I wanted so badly to engage him, but I was dehydrated and starving. Thankfully, my mother noticed I was slowly slipping into a coma.

"All of them," my mom said.

The waiter, intrigued by us, leaned in closer.

"Is that close to New York City?"

My mom picked up her menu and began to browse the first few pages. "Very close."

The waiter reached across the table to realign the salt and pepper shakers. "My sister went on a trip to America recently," he said. "She liked it very much."

"Oh, great. Which state?" my mom asked.

"Mexico."

My mom and I snickered because one of the observations we had made while traveling is that, despite what we're told by the U.S. media, most of the world is not as keenly focused on our part of the planet.

"I know we've been away for a few days, but I didn't realize the U.S. had acquired a new state," I said.

The waiter smiled. "I know. It's a crazy world."

"Yes, I suppose it is."

The waiter took a small notepad and pen from his apron pocket and prepared himself to take our order.

"Do you serve wine here?" asked my mom.

"Yes, ma'am. We are permitted to serve alcohol here."

I'm embarrassed to admit it, but after hearing the waiter's response I felt a surge of elation rise through my body.

"Oh, thank God," my mom said. "I'll take a glass of chardonnay." She moved her gaze to me and caught me nodding in agreement. "Make that two," she added.

"Okay. Two glasses of charldonnay."

My mother looked puzzled. "No. *Chardonnay*," she corrected him.

"Yes, of course," he replied. "Two glasses of charldonnay."

My mother wasn't one to fixate on a mispronunciation, but to her mispronouncing *chardonnay* was akin to blasphemy.

"I'm sorry, but you're mispronouncing *chardonnay*," she explained. "Chardonnay is a fabulous wine enjoyed all over the world. How are we supposed to be friends if you can't pronounce my favorite refreshment?"

To the waiter's credit, he looked sincerely interested in getting the pronunciation right. I hoped it wasn't because of my mother's friend request. I didn't want to pass judgment on him too quickly, but she'd eat him alive within the first hour.

"Charrrr-donnnn-ay," she said, exaggerating each syllable. Chardonnay!"

"Charl-donnn-ay," the waiter said, trying to mimic my mom.

"Chardonnay," she repeated, gently encouraging him.

As my mother continued her audiology session with the waiter, I was taken back to my early teens when my mother's mission to save the world, or at least our neighborhood, began to ramp up. I'm not exaggerating when I say that at one time or another we housed nearly every other teenager on our street. When Kelly's closest friend fought with her parents, my mom would invite her to crash on our couch until the dust settled, which on one occasion lasted two years. When my brother's friend Jimmy ran away from home because he was "misunderstood," my mom happily cleared an area of our basement to make room for a cot. Despite all of the squatters, I didn't truly understand the intensity of my mother's desire to help others until she began to hold office hours. She'd set aside a few hours one evening a week to allow kids from the neighborhood to stop by, crack open a can of soda or eat leftovers, and unload all of their adolescent baggage. My mother's history of altruism was the reason I wasn't fazed by her fixation on coaching our waiter on the proper pronunciation of her favorite beverage.

The waiter tried again. "Charldonnay!"

"You are so cute," my mom said. "But there's no L in chardonnay."

The waiter's face lit up. "Oh! Chardonnay! Chardonnay!"

"Yes!" my mom yelled, visibly excited by the waiter's accomplishment. "That's it." She jumped out of her seat and gave the waiter a big hug. "My hope has been restored." The waiter was absolutely delighted.

"The fun's not going to stop here," I said, "because when you come back we'll teach you how to say *lorazepam* and *irritable bowel syndrome*."

The waiter blushed and hurried off to get our drinks. "You do realize that he'll be saying *chardonnay* over and over again for the rest of the day," I said.

"Then my work here is done."

We spent the next hour sipping our wine and solving the world's problems. There aren't many problems you can't solve with a glass of chardonnay and a halfway decent conversationalist. Almost immediately after my mom and I balanced the U.S. budget and just prior to dismantling both sides of the debate on global warming, I caught the waiter's attention and signaled to him that we were ready for another glass of wine. He walked behind the bar and past the shelf that held the wine bottles and disappeared through a doorway. A moment later, he emerged with two glasses of white wine.

That's strange, I thought. *Where is that wine coming from?* "Can I see the bottle you're pouring this wine from?" I asked him when he arrived at our table.

The waiter fumbled through his response in what appeared to be part Arabic or Urdu (I couldn't tell) and waved his arms in the air as if to suggest he didn't understand.

"Cut the crap," I said. I didn't want to offend my mom's newest friend, but my curiosity about the wine's source was getting the best of me. "We just listened to a fifteen-minute conversation between you and the host about American football. And it was in perfect English. Please go get the bottle."

The waiter conceded and marched away toward the back room. He emerged with a small cardboard box. As he walked toward us, I realized what he was holding.

"Boxed wine?" I shouted.

"Yes, of course," he replied. "It's our house wine. It's a very good brand."

My mother took a sip of her wine and shrugged in approval.

"Even the label implies it's bad," I said. The tag line on the box read: "Good wine when you're in a pinch."

Side note: I have a group of friends who would stop talking to me if they discovered I'd been drinking boxed wine.

"It's very good," the waiter assured me.

"Take a look around," I said. "Does it look like we're in a pinch?"

"Well, we *are* in an Islamic country, David," my mom said. "I'd call that a pinch."

I looked up at the waiter. "Are my lips swelling? They're starting to tingle."

"You look fine to me," he replied.

I started to breathe heavily and pat my cheeks. "Are you sure my face isn't swelling?" I continued my antics for several minutes hoping to get the reaction I wanted.

The waiter looked down at me without the slightest sign of empathy. "Sir, I remember you from previous visits. This is the same wine you've been drinking all along."

I dropped my head into my hands. "There is such a thing as late-onset allergic reaction. A caring person would show some empathy. I'm clearly in distress."

The waiter reached for my glass of wine. "Shall I take it away?"

I grabbed his hand and looked up at him. "Let's not get ahead of ourselves. Let's see how this plays out."

The waiter rolled his eyes and walked away.

My mother grabbed a handful of peanuts from a bowl the waiter had placed on our table when we first sat down and popped a few into her mouth. "You know, I've been serving you boxed wine for years," she confessed.

"Not right now, Mother. If you haven't noticed, I have a lot to absorb, and I don't need the added stress."

She leaned back in her chair and dropped the remaining peanuts into her mouth. "Anxiety really is your secret weapon, because I'm friggin' exhausted."

I grabbed my own handful of peanuts. "Well, then *my* work here is done."

CHAPTER 23

All the Single Ladies

The following morning I had every intention of sleeping in. I was still suffering from the side effects of having drunk boxed wine, and the prior day's adventure at the bank had wiped me out. At about 7 A.M. a young Filipino man, Timmy, from the housekeeping staff knocked on my door. I knew Timmy from my previous stays at the hotel because he was often the one who cleaned my room.

"Houthkeepie," Timmy called through the closed door.

I forgot to mention he has a slight speech impediment. I sat up and lifted my eyeshades. Before I was able to get out of bed to open the door, Timmy barged into the room.

"In case you hadn't noticed, I placed the Do Not Disturb sign on my door."

Timmy walked over to the window and opened the curtains. "You thleep too much. Three day I no clean room. Not healthy."

The bright morning sunshine forced me to squint.

"I have everything I need, Timmy."

"No. I change towel, clean bathroom, and fold laundry."

"Triple threat, huh? Who are you, Beyoncé?"

Timmy turned to me. His face lit up like a kid's on Christmas morning. "Bee-yon-thee!" he cried. He dropped his cleaning towel onto the floor and broke into a rendition of "All the Single Ladies."

I took my eyeshades off. "Oh, wow! You're really getting into it."

Timmy hunched over and threw his fists toward the floor while he slowly backed up.

"Whoa, you even have her signature move down."

Timmy continued dancing. I watched for a few minutes, hoping that each fist pump would be his last. As the song went on, he got more into it. I hadn't intended to see a full performance, and I started to wonder whether I might need to move the ironing board out of his way. Timmy danced his way to the edge of the bed and picked something up from the nightstand.

"'If you liked it, then you thoulda put a ring on it.'"

I jumped out of bed. "Hey, wait!" I shouted. "That's not a ring. That's my mouth guard."

Timmy rocked on, completely oblivious.

"Whoa, dude! That was a full split right on the carpet." The situation was getting awkward.

Timmy spun away from me and crossed the room in what I can only describe as a sashay. When he stopped, he turned his head back toward me and placed his hands on his hips.

"All the thingle ladyth!" He stood there breathing hard, apparently waiting for a reaction from me. I was more than happy to oblige.

"I'm sorry, it's a no for me. There were some real pitch problems from the start, and I felt your dance moves were predictable. Maybe you'll have better luck next year."

Timmy's face fell. He clearly was not happy with my feedback.

I hated to be the bad guy, but I felt I owed him an honest response. There's a reason people who can't sing audition for reality singing competitions: no one gives them honest feedback. Timmy didn't deserve that fate.

He looked stricken. "I go clean bathroom now."

I was now officially awake. Rather than lie in bed listening to Timmy hum through Beyoncé's entire discology, I got up and put some clothes on. Timmy stayed for another half an hour. After he left, I sat down at the small desk and began sifting through work emails. I barely got through two emails when there was a knock on my door. When I opened the door, my mom and sister pushed their way into the room. They, too, were wide awake and had decided to see what kind of trouble I was getting into.

"Good morning," my mom said as she walked past me.

Kelly walked over to the small sofa next to the bed and sat down. "It's our last full day here. The trip flew by so fast."

I sat down on the edge of the bed. "That's because you didn't join us at the bank yesterday. I equate that experience to having my toenails slowly cut out with a rusty butter knife." My mom nodded in agreement. Another knock came at the door. My mom answered it. It was the young woman who had stopped by earlier that week.

"Oh, Jesus, it's you again?" I said in jest. The woman stepped past my mom and into the room.

"Hi, Mr. David. It's nice to see you again."

"Mmmm-hmmm," I replied.

The woman flipped through her notebook. "I can see here that you've requested no children and no interruptions."

"I'm glad to see you're using your notes effectively," I replied.

She dismissed my comment and said, "I wanted to let you know that the youth leadership program we discussed previously will be utilizing this floor of the hotel all day. There will likely be noise disturbances."

I stood up and walked toward her. "I have two million reward points with this hotel. I'm willing to hand them over right now if you designate this floor as a no-child zone." I wasn't joking this time.

"That's interesting," she replied. "Didn't you yell at me last time I was here?"

"I wouldn't call that yelling. It was more like an aggressive propulsion of air across my vocal chords."

The woman walked back to the door and turned around. "While I'm here, are you in need of any service items?"

"Bath salts," I replied.

"You want to go there again, huh? Okay, game on." She stepped out of the room, then turned to face us. "Oh, I heard you drank boxed wine last night."

I whipped my head around to face my mother. She shrugged and forced an apologetic look onto her face.

"Wait! You two know each other?"

"Yes," replied the woman. We had a great conversation last night in the lounge downstairs." She pointed to my mother. "This woman is awesome. And do *we* have a surprise for you."

"But—" My twisted tongue got the best of me. I tried to say something, anything, but couldn't. I wanted to know more about the surprise they had cooked up. But it was too late.

"Buh-bye," the woman sang as she closed the door.

I turned my attention to the woman who had thrown me under the bus the previous night. "Really, Mom? You told her about the boxed wine?" There were some things a mother absolutely should never do to her gay son. Squealing to others that he may or may not have drunk boxed wine was in the top two or three, for sure.

"You drank boxed wine?" Kelly asked. "I thought she was joking."

My mom sat down next to my sister and stared up at me. "It just sort of slipped out."

Side note: Just off the top of my head, I can think of a few obvious things that just "slip out." Diaphragms. Tongue rings. Evil thoughts about your mother-in-law. Notice that I didn't short-list boxed wine.

"My life is ruined now. Thank you."

"Oh, calm down. A little boxed wine never hurt anyone. Look what it's done for me."

I sat down on the bed and placed my hands on my lower abdomen. "I think I'm gonna be sick."

My mom jumped up and sat next to me. "Remember that conversation we had on that tiny plane in Costa Rica? You and I are a lot alike. You need to embrace that."

"That nun in Catholic school was right. I should have diverted more energy into prayer. This is my punishment."

"You really drank boxed wine?" Kelly asked again.

"We were in a pinch," I snapped.

I stretched out on the bed and stared at the ceiling. I tried to regulate my breathing and erase the previous twenty-four hours from my memory. My meditation was soon interrupted by yet another knock on the door. No one moved. After the second knock, I got up and opened the door. Standing in front of me were at least twenty children, all huddled into a semicircle. A young girl in the front row who was sporting short pigtails and had a lotus flower poking out from behind her left ear began to sing. The rest of the group followed as they entered into the first verse of "We are the World." My mom and Kelly joined me at the door. *That darn leadership program*, I thought. *This was the surprise they had planned for me.* The song went on for what seemed like an eternity. The song had several more verses than Dionne Warwick and her friends had led us to believe. As the group of children carried the last note to completion, I noticed the diminutive program leader standing right smack in the middle of the group. When we made eye contact, she smiled at me and tried not to laugh. I winked at her.

"What did you think?" asked the woman. The children stood quietly and gazed at me, almost as if they were trying to guess what I might say. I was in a real pickle. I saw only two logical options: option A, which was to say something sweet and encouraging to the kids, or option B, which was to blurt out exactly what was on my mind.

"Someone in there was singing way out of tune." Several of the kids booed and whispered in disapproval. "I didn't say it was one of you kids."

Side note: In case it wasn't obvious from my last remark, I chose option A.

"Nice," replied the woman.

Although I got a kick from teasing the woman, whose name I later found out was Lena, I thoroughly enjoyed the performance and her sense of humor. I hadn't felt that alive in a long time. The world had always seemed so big to me, but there I was, a long way from home, using humor to connect with people I may never have had the chance to meet had I not traveled. All of the trips my mom and I had taken finally made sense. They had a purpose. I felt incredibly fortunate, and I didn't want the moment to end. But it did. After the applause subsided, each of the children gave my mom a hug, high-fived my sister and me, and then scurried down the hall.

"Those kids were so darn cute," my mom said. "That will be a great story for my friends back home." She closed the door and walked back to take her seat next to my sister.

"What's on the agenda for today?" Kelly asked.

I was just about to offer my suggestion when my mom said, "Well, now that we're all together and alone, there's something I want to share with you."

I walked back to the bed and sat down. There was something about the tone of her voice that made me believe the "something" she wanted to share was not good. My normal reaction would have been to assault her with a million questions, but I held back. I sensed that this conversation was going to be different. I looked at my mom and saw what I hoped I would never see. Fear. I've seen my mother freak out before, but the look on her face wasn't the same one she has when we hit turbulence or when a bartender yells, "Last call." The look on her face told a much different story. She was truly scared.

CHAPTER 24

The Silver Lining

"I have breast cancer."

It happened just like that. My mom shared her secret without an anesthetic or an attempt to soften the blow. She told us that she had cancer as if she were telling us she had calloused feet. She continued talking for a few minutes more, but I didn't hear any of it. All I heard was *cancer*. I was speechless. I didn't know what to do. I felt angry and sad, but more so scared and desperate. Most of all, I felt betrayed. The betrayal I felt wasn't on the same scale as the betrayal I experienced earlier when I discovered that my mom had told a complete stranger that I had drunk boxed wine. This feeling of betrayal was far deeper because I felt betrayed by life itself. I was being forced to accept that my mother was human, vulnerable. How could that be? She was my superhero. A bubble of emotion rose in my throat, so I retreated to where I felt comfortable, the land of a million questions. How long has she known? What stage was she in? What was her prognosis? Was she going to live?

I hoped Kelly would find an opening to take control of the conversation and begin flushing out the facts. I knew I couldn't fill that role. Not right then. My mind had been hijacked. I found myself consumed by thoughts of the past. All of the memories my mom and I had created over the past forty years flashed through my mind in an instant, and all I could think about was that we hadn't done enough. There had to be more time, more memories to create. With only those four words my mother had shared with us, I was reduced to being a child again. I wanted to throw my arms around my mom and cry, like I did when I was a kid, and tell her that I loved her and that she didn't need to be scared. I wanted her to know how I felt, that she wasn't alone. We would go through this together, like we always had. Then a surge of guilt came over me. I felt embarrassed about all the times I had exaggerated my ailments and drew attention to myself by claiming I was on the verge of death. My mother's situation was real. She could *actually* die.

And then a thought came out of nowhere and hit me like a freight train. *Wait a minute. My mom doesn't have breasts.* I was certain. Well, I take that back. I wasn't entirely certain because several years earlier I watched my mom as she unsuccessfully attempted to conceal herself behind a napkin in Costa Rica. But, to be honest, I had done such a wonderful job erasing those few moments from my memory that I couldn't recall actually seeing her breasts. I know Pete and I talked briefly about a possible nipple sighting, but I wasn't prepared to undo six months of intense therapy to recreate the events of that night. It was far more calming to assume that it didn't matter that her aim was off. Then I shifted my thoughts to my childhood when bullies repeatedly drove me into my mother's arms, and not once did I recall feeling the cushioning of an endowed chest. I was by no means an expert on the topic, but I'd like to think I could tell the difference between padding and no padding. Even as thousands of images of my mom flashed through my mind, there wasn't a single one that definitively proved my mom had breasts. That likely explained why she didn't know where to place that cocktail napkin. Her ill-placed napkin wasn't intentional after all! All of this made sense now. My mother's diagnosis was a big mistake. I was now sure of it. Finally, I was ready to respond.

"Don't you need breasts to get breast cancer?"

"David?" screamed Kelly. "You can't joke about this." She stared at me with her mouth wide open in disbelief. She's never shared our "go big or go home" approach to life.

"That was exactly my thought," my mom replied. "When they told me they found a suspicious spot on my mammogram, I assumed they had found a nipple."

I was relieved my mother responded the way she did. Otherwise, I could easily have been labeled the worst son ever.

"Surprisingly," she said. "I have breasts after all."

"Well, maybe that's the silver lining in all of this," I replied. Kelly was still speechless.

"That's one way of looking a it," my mom replied.

There was a painfully long silence after my mom spoke. Each of us looked around the room and at each other. My sister fiddled with the piping on the couch cushions while I doodled on the notepad next to the phone. My mother finally broke the silence by laughing. Maybe it was a result of complete exhaustion or the relief of getting that secret out in the open, but she laughed so hard that she could barely catch her breath. She fell back onto the bed, holding her stomach while she wheezed and snorted. Kelly and I joined in. When I started laughing, I couldn't stop. Just when I thought I had myself under control, my mother would start laughing again or I would catch a glimpse of my sister, and off I would go. We nearly laughed ourselves unconscious.

I think we needed the comic relief; I know I did. Once the laughter subsided, my sister and I were able to ask the million questions that were on our mind. The cancer had been caught early. The prognosis was good. Treatment was to start the following month. There was so much to talk about, and I knew it wouldn't all be settled in that room, but we talked for hours anyway. By the time we finished talking it was early afternoon, and we were beyond exhausted. My mother suggested that we use the remaining time together to see the tourist sites we had missed before we had to return to the hotel and prepare for our flight home.

We spent the remainder of the day visiting the Burj Khalifa, the Jumeirah Mosque, and Burj Al Arab, where we had afternoon tea. We wandered through the narrow alleys of the gold and spice souks and finished the day with a dhow boat dinner cruise in Dubai Marina. I'm glad we ventured out of my hotel room that day because the sight-seeing turned out to be a perfect distraction, and we had a wonderful time together.

We arrived back at the hotel around 11:30 P.M. Our flight didn't leave for a few more hours, so we returned to our rooms to pack our bags. I finished fairly quickly and dragged my luggage to the lobby to wait for my mom and sister. The lobby was empty, so I spread out my things on a couch in the far corner across from the hotel's bar and opened my laptop. My mind was still spinning from the news about my mom, but I jumped into some work anyway. I still needed a distraction. A few moments later, a young girl, maybe nine or ten, walked over and took a seat in a chair next to the couch.

"So what's your story?" she asked with a degree of casualness and confidence that one might expect from someone three or four times her age. I looked up from my laptop. She had shoulder-length blond hair and pudgy, rose-colored cheeks. Her hair was flipped back behind her ears. A small barrette in the shape of a gerber daisy pinned the hair on her left side into place.

"I don't have a story."

"It's late at night and you're in an empty hotel lobby in Dubai. There has to be a story here."

She seemed sure there was something more to my being alone in the lobby. I looked down at my laptop and continued working. I wasn't in the mood for conversation. After the day I had, I craved the solace of mindless spreadsheets and emails.

The girl didn't pick up on my closed body language. "So what do you do?"

"I eat unattended children."

The girl, unaffected by my comment, kicked off her flip-flops and put her feet up on the table in front of us. "Cute."

"What do you do?" I asked. I was annoyed that I was being pulled into the conversation, so I was purposefully sarcastic in my response.

The girl looked at me with contempt. "I'm ten. I don't do anything."

"Where are your parents?"

The girl rolled her eyes and pointed to the bar area across the lobby. "Frank and Georgette are at the bar."

"Smart parents."

The girl looked toward the bar for a moment longer before returning her attention to me. "You look tired."

I don't know what it was about that girl. Maybe it was the casualness with which she engaged me or the confidence in her voice. I couldn't put my finger on it. I admitted to her that I was tired. I probably sounded defensive as I described the responsibility I had at work and at home. I also told her that someone close to me was not well and how heavy that was weighing on me. Although I didn't intend to get sucked into a conversation, I was in it. She asked two or three more questions about my life and about the person who was sick. I told her that I felt helpless and that part of me would prefer to consume myself with work rather than deal with the days, weeks, and months ahead and that I felt guilty for feeling that way. *Why am I sharing all of this?* I thought. She was pushing me too far.

"It's your mom, isn't it?" Her tone of voice made the hair on my arms rise.

"Yes."

The girl's cell phone beeped. She picked it up from the coffee table and checked it.

"You carry yourself quite well for your age," I told her.

"I get that a lot," she said without looking up.

I felt that I had shared too much. The conversation needed to end before I broke down. "Aren't Frank and Georgette looking for you?"

"I have time." She shifted her gaze to the bar. "Georgette drinks two glasses of wine. She's still on her second." The girl picked up a magazine from the table and flipped through it casually. "Interesting."

"What's interesting?" I asked, now fully engaged.

She plopped the magazine onto the coffee table. "Nothing. I'm just curious why adults overcomplicate stuff. You have a lot of responsibility. Big deal. Lots of people have responsibility at work." She glanced over at the bar and then stood up and slipped into her flip-flops. "I gotta bounce," she said. She took a step and then stopped. "Don't work so hard. Connecting with people is far more interesting. Besides, people who work too hard have children like me."

I raised my eyebrows to prompt her to finish.

"Unattended," she said. And with that she was gone.

Side note: That girl may have been only ten, but she had read me like I was yesterday's news.

Why that girl had sat down next to me and engaged me in a conversation remains a mystery, but I was glad she did. I needed someone to hold a mirror up to me and prevent me from making a serious mistake. I didn't need to spend more of my time on work. I needed to focus on the people in my life who were important to me. Those are the people who would be there, in person or in spirit, long after the work was gone. That young girl had just given me an incredible gift.

"You ready?"

My mom's voice startled me. I hadn't seen her approach me.

"Where's Kelly?" Just as I asked the question I caught a glimpse of my sister standing outside the lobby doors.

"She's outside getting a cab for us."

I stood up, shoved my laptop into my knapsack, and pulled my suitcase out from behind the couch. "I'm ready."

My mom turned toward the lobby door. I touched her arm. She stopped. "Mom, I'm sorry this is happening to you. You don't deserve it."

She turned back to me and gave me a hug. "Cancer happens to the good ones, David. I know I'll be fine." She let go of me and backed up so that we faced each other. She looked relaxed.

"Yes, you will," I replied.

I noticed my sister waving to us outside. Our taxi had arrived. My mom saw her, too, and motioned me on. "I'll tell you what," I said. "Let's get you back to good health, and then I'll take you on another adventure. Sound good?"

"Get out your credit card. We're going to Italy."

I didn't have a crystal ball to tell me that my mom and I would make it to Italy, but I felt we would. I knew we'd get there, and I couldn't wait. My mom was heading toward the exit. I caught up with her.

"Hey, Mom, I was thinking, would this be an inappropriate time to put dibs on the painting that's hanging in your dining room, the one I love so much?"

In her classic style she responded without missing a beat. "I'm leaving that painting to my favorite child. I guess you'll just have to wait and see who that is." She stepped through the exit and handed her suitcase to the taxi driver. As she stooped to climb into the backseat of the taxi next to my sister, she turned her head and looked up at me. "And it's going to be a long wait."

AFTERWARD

In case you're wondering, Mom is doing well. Her treatment was successful, and she's been cancer-free for several years now. Since our trip to Dubai, she partly retired, which means she's busier now than she was when she worked full-time. When she does have free time, she and my stepdad visit with my sister Kelly, her husband, and their three children, mostly to give Kelly an opportunity to speak with other adults and to help her move beyond the grunting.

Pete and I were able to visit Italy with my mom. Despite the fact that we spent nearly half of our vacation driving around the base of the Leaning Tower of Pisa looking for, of all things, the Leaning Tower of Pisa, we had a delightful time. Upon our return, I was forced to undergo a two-week liver cleanse, and Pete is still sifting through the three hundred gigabytes of pictures my mother took, but the trip was well worth it. I smell another book!